pattern

orla kiely

conran
OCTOPUS

• • • • • • • • •

To Bob and Maeve — with love

• • • • • • • • •

contents

introduction

· · · · · · · · ·

As a little girl I was mesmerized by pattern. I would find myself tracing undulating swirls of organic forms, scrutinizing them to discover where the motif eventually repeated itself. Following these forms as they spiralled across a surface, I would squint my eyes to see how new patterns appeared – where denser areas created stripes or checks, and where abstract shapes appeared in the less cluttered open spaces as the pattern blurred.

I sometimes think that my brain works in repeat. I love the order and regiment of repetition, and how anything and everything can be patterned in this way, as if you are looking at the world through a prism or kaleidoscope. It is something that is very beautiful and inspiring to me.

Growing up in Ireland in the late 1960s and early 1970s was intrinsic to my creative DNA. Our family home, where I lived throughout my formative years, was a modern 1950s-style house. One of my most vivid memories is of our family kitchen with its olive-green Formica cupboards and worktops, coordinating green and white patterned tiles – full wall coverage – and to top it off an orange gloss ceiling – I loved it.

We lived two minutes from the sea and although it often rained I spent a lot of time outdoors – on the beach or in the fields, with the mountains close by. My taste for colour has been influenced by my childhood – my love for green, from moss to seaweed, the greys and browns of the huge skies and rolling landscapes, the mustard yellow of gorse on the hills and the wild flowers on the roadside verges. It is hard to believe now that this was suburban Dublin.

My love of fashion was also evident from a very early age. I got my first sewing machine when I was 12 and became absorbed with making things. Later, fashion would become my window to the world, a way to voice my personal language, and to communicate my ideas.

Throughout my career I have experimented with many styles and influences, working on various jobs and projects, and have come to realize that I am happiest doing my own work. The kind of experience that I gained in my early working life was crucial in the development of my personal style and helped me to identify my likes and dislikes, and to understand when an idea was good, when to stop, when to go on. The kind of training I received was all about finding solutions, solving puzzles, forming an individual aesthetic. It was a great foundation or building block for a life in design.

With my own label, I have always followed my instincts. I firmly believe that being true to yourself is a guarantee that quality and integrity will shine through. What motivates me is the possibility that my work can give pleasure and be uplifting. Our aim was always to be accessible and to be creative in the fullest sense of the word. What I like most is that my work is identifiable; it has established its own handwriting and stands out as mine. Over time, while it may have changed, developed and evolved, it can't help but retain its individuality. It has always been about my personal expression and take on the world.

Fashion is both fascinating and contradictory. It creates trends and follows them, it welcomes and rejects; it judges. I love the fact that I am part of it but I also relish the knowledge that my design language is different. I can be an outsider. Incapable of following trends just for the sake of it, I'm not in the business of reinventing myself to be this year's sensation. My need is to feel both inspired and satisfied by what I achieve. I do my own thing. I love fashion but I would never want to be its slave.

Recalling my early days as a student and then graduate designer, the world of fashion and textiles relied on skills, such as creative drawing, painting and draughtsmanship. In simple words, no technology. Every idea for a design had to be considered, sketched and thought through before committing to the time-consuming task of manually painting up a large-scale artwork. One mistake and the work would be compromised.

Early on in my career, during my first design position at Esprit, I was exposed to the potential of computers while working alongside the in-house team of graphic designers. I was amazed at how quickly you could switch a colour, a line or an element, and make the pattern bigger or smaller. Even so, I also realized that visualization and forethought were still vital. Without that, you might churn out endless possibilities or permutations for a mediocre result. Today the team of talented, spirited and like-minded young designers, who work alongside me in our studio, rely (as I do) on technology as an important tool. A computer cannot design for you.

Although our label started with bags, I have always designed for fashion. However a design looked on paper, it always came alive on cloth. The crispness or sturdiness of cotton, the shimmer and drape of silk, the depth and warmth of wool, I loved it all. When working as a young designer I found it disheartening to see some of my work translated into garments I would never wear or simply didn't care for. While my taste has evolved through the decades, certain elements have been constant. My style is clean, simple, measured, bold and brave. I believe in committing oneself fully to a design without compromise.

What is essential in my approach is to be very observant with a sharp eye for detail. Details, no matter how subtle, can make all the difference. My fussiness frustrates even me on occasions. The shape of a collar, the size of a pocket, the quality of thread, the exactness of colour are all worth bothering about.

My boredom threshold is very low and I have an underlying need to refresh everything I do. Our Stem print is a good example of this. Ever since its first outing in 2000 we realized that it was special. It had a simple graphic strength and charm. Everyone wanted it. But I quickly realized that it would have to change and develop or it would simply peter out.

I love the surprise of the unexpected, the chance happening that is part and parcel of the design process. Like many designers, influences can creep up on me. I can fall in love with an idea instantly; equally, I might come round to concepts I have previously dismissed. I also believe that it is never too late to alter or modify a design, even if it's the final hour, whatever opposition you might face. After all, we have to look and live with the consequences. The emotional high of a successful design or product is well worth fighting for.

I am very lucky. While it has taken sheer hard work to get to this point, somehow, throughout my education and experience, early career opportunities and whatever else, I have managed to make my passion into my career. Together with my husband and business partner, we have come through the challenges of starting, seeding and building our brand.

Pattern is not a trend for me, to be taken up one minute and abandoned the next when the winds of fashion change. Pattern is in me. It is my life.

Overleaf: Stem print blanket from S/S 2007 location shoot.

13

life

starting out

· · · · · · · · ·

With hindsight, it can be tempting to see a pattern in past events that might not have been there, or to make out a clear path forward where one was not so obvious at the time. Yet, looking back, it was always apparent to me from an early age that art was going to play some sort of role in my life – as a child, I was always doodling away. I enjoyed art and my teachers' compliments encouraged me to think that I was good at it; at the same time, what interested me most was working in a stylized, graphic way with shapes and colours, which has never changed. My instincts have always led me in the direction of design rather than what one might call fine art.

Another one of my childhood enthusiasms was for making things. I loved to sew and to select fabrics to make up the patterns. By the time I was 12, I would happily make clothes for myself and my younger sisters. We still laugh about some of the creations I inflicted upon my youngest sister, Nessa. Knitting was another pastime that I enjoyed, and I completed a number of stripy sweaters, although I always found progress a little slow. Crocheting, on the other hand, was satisfying and fast. I remember making crocheted waistcoats when I was very young, patching the squares together. All in quite mad colours.

I grew up in a quiet, leafy suburb on the outskirts of Dublin, Ireland. The area was still quite undeveloped in those days, and there were fields and green spaces all around. The big expanses of sky and sea, the freshness of the wind and the sound of seagulls are nostalgic memories for me.

Childhood photographs from the family album.

There were four of us – my older brother, myself and my two younger sisters – and we all got on well with each other. At least part of the reason for that lack of sibling friction must be to do with the fact that our parents encouraged us to develop our own individual strengths. In my brother's case, for example, it was languages. Both of my parents had gone to university in the 1950s and my mother had worked as a scientist in the state laboratory before they were married. It was an unfortunate sign of the times that as soon as she became engaged, it was made clear to her by her employers that she should consider her career to be over, which would be unthinkable nowadays.

Both my grandmothers were strong and interesting women. My father's mother was a businesswoman and the matriarch of the family. My mother's mother was very creative in a down-to-earth, practical sort of way – oil painting, cooking, making cheese. I like to think that I owe some of my creativity to her, along with my desire and determination to start projects and finish them.

Back then, all schools in Ireland were religious schools and there was little choice when it came to education. Strange as it may seem now, I spent my entire schooling, from the age of 4 to the age of 18, attending the same convent as a day pupil. It was a Loreto convent – the Sisters of Loreto, a fact I discovered later, being a branch of an order originally founded by an Englishwoman called Mary Ward, who believed women should be educated on an equal basis to men.

At school we were urged to do well, while at home my parents always encouraged us to believe that we could achieve independence through education. A notable influence on me was my art teacher, who was

Dusseldorf 1986, photograph taken while working at Esprit.

particularly supportive of me and a real mentor. She was a sweet, eccentric nun, who seemed very old to me but was probably only middle-aged at the time. Much later, when I was accepted to do a master's degree at the Royal College of Art in London, England, she sent me a lovely letter saying how proud she was of me.

As the time approached for my final exams, the question was what to do next. While art college was a natural choice for further education, the other possibility I was thinking about was architecture. Eventually, with my teacher's encouragement, I applied to the National College of Art and Design in Dublin, otherwise known as the NCAD. It was, at that time, the best college out of three and quite hard to get into, and I was somewhat daunted by the prospect of submitting my portfolio. Yet despite the fact that there were others in the art class who I thought were much better at drawing, I was the only one who was accepted, perhaps because they liked my use of colour or perhaps because my portfolio showed an interest in fashion, which might have been considered focused.

A good foundation year at art school should open up new worlds and possibilities to students and introduce them to techniques and disciplines they had never considered before. The foundation course at the NCAD was excellent. We'd spend short periods of six weeks or so exploring different aspects of artistic work and practice in rotation, during which time I discovered an aptitude for graphics, and that, within textiles, weaving didn't appeal to me at all because it was so slow and time-consuming.

After foundation, we embarked on the three-year BA course. By the end of my foundation year I knew that I wanted to focus on textiles, so I joined the fashion and textile department, specializing in print. We were

Illustrations, print swatches and photographs from my degree collection at NCAD.

a close class, only five of us, and the technicians who assisted us were very helpful and supportive. The whole process of mixing colours, exposing screens and printing appealed to me enormously: it was very rewarding seeing the results so quickly. My focus was creating printed fabric for use in fashion, rather than furnishings, although in retrospect my student work – which even then was very graphic, clean and stylized – would have been very relevant for interior spaces.

My three-year course in Print for Fashion ended with our fashion show. For the first time all five print students showed their work. Looking back, I think we stole the show, with all the national papers reporting on the textile students, much to the chagrin of the fashion department.

After graduation I decided to go to New York with my good friend Jane to gain work experience. We joined another friend, Paula, who was already there. Leaving Ireland immediately after college to go to New York may sound like a bold and confident step, but like many young Irish people at the time I knew I would have to travel to find a good design position.

New York in the mid-1980s was a thrilling place, and although my parents occasionally expressed concern about me cycling around the East Village on my bicycle, I was having great fun rummaging around in vintage shops, going to parties and spending time with other friends from Ireland in what seemed to me to be the coolest of cities. The original Barney's, a beautiful department store between West 17th Street and 7th Avenue, was a favourite haunt of mine, and was probably the first store I really noticed and was inspired by in a fashion context. The collections they stocked and the visual merchandising was very fashion-forward and very different to anything in Dublin.

Thanks to Paula, we had somewhere to live – a sublet in Chelsea on 21st Street between 7th and 8th Avenues – and we were both offered jobs in the same design company she worked for, which was rather like an American version of Habitat. There I gained the best colour training anyone could possibly have had.

In those pre-digital days, everything had to be done by hand. My immediate boss, a woman who designed the tiny coordinated patterns for wallpaper and fabric for which the company was well-known, would give me a palette of colours and I would have to mix the sample pots of gouache in order to paint up final designs for presentations. These colours had to be mixed perfectly to match the originals. Once the sample pots were prepared, the colours would be painstakingly brushed onto card and dried with a hairdryer. 'Not dirty enough' would be her comment, or 'make it cleaner'. Often her suggestion was 'add Linden green', which I will always remember. Then I would have to try again, gradually learning how to mix the colours by eye. Afterward, it was a case of painting the paper artwork, or *croquis*. Again, it was meticulous, exacting work, painting in the patterns by hand using the finest, tiniest of brushes, or drawing very controlled lines with a ruling pen. All the different colourways of each pattern had to be painted in this way. The next stage was putting all the designs into repeat, copying and pasting the patterns together to build a big enough piece to view from a distance. This was how we could see if a repeat was working.

To earn some extra money, we took on freelance projects as well, working at night and sometimes at the weekends. (I learned another valuable but painful lesson when I spent a week working on a big artwork and

Overleaf: Friends from Esprit days (left) and a top featuring one of my prints (right).

subsequently lost it on the subway.) Although the work was, in a sense, technical, there was a creative element to the decision-making that went into it. Because everything had to be painted by hand, you had to make choices early on with a degree of confidence, otherwise you might end up spending a day painting something only to find that it was not quite right and have to start over.

After a year, I was quite keen to move on, and so I left New York together with my two friends. We spent a couple of months back in Dublin updating our portfolios before leaving for London to find a job. Luckily we all did – mine was at Esprit, an American fashion company, which was based in Dusseldorf, Germany.

The company was a good fit for me. It was creative and interesting and I liked the graphic style for which they were noted at the time. There were three of us responsible for designing print, working on designs across the full range of womenswear, menswear and childrenswear, presenting our ideas to the head designers. Within two months of arriving at Dusseldorf I was travelling to Singapore and Hong Kong as part of the fashion team, so that I could be on the spot to tweak and fix the prints the moment they came off the table. I stayed in Germany for two years, made good friends and travelled a good deal. (My parents' concern over me cycling had by now given way to worries about me driving on autobahns on the right-hand side.) In retrospect, I suppose I was quietly ambitious. We had to be. It was not easy at that time to find employment in print design, and jobs in fashion were also thin on the ground.

The years at Esprit, which also included another two years based in London travelling to Dusseldorf for meetings, gave me invaluable experience.

As a print designer, however, I was beginning to want a greater degree of control – the fashion team could ask for a print to be changed and you would have to go ahead and change it, whether you thought that was a good idea or not. Rather than look for another job for a similar company, I decided on a shift of direction and applied to the Royal College.

The Royal College of Art in London is the only dedicated postgraduate school of art and design in the world, and being accepted to study for an MA there was an exciting moment for me. Although I had had a good deal of work experience (and the portfolio to prove it), I was still young enough to enjoy my time there and two years passed by very quickly.

While my first degree had focused on graphics and print design, at the Royal College I decided to specialize in knitwear. Getting to grips with machine knitting meant learning a great deal technically, but it also brought another dimension to my design work, which proved very valuable. It was an interesting and absorbing time, made possible for me financially by the support of my father and my future husband, Dermott Rowan, along with a certain amount of belt-tightening.

The culmination of every art student's college life and work is the final degree show. As part of my final collection I designed a range of hats made from handmade felt, colourful wool fibres needle-punched onto a backing of gingham. This fabric was the result of experiments that I had made using the huge needle-puncher at Huddersfield College in Yorkshire, a machine chiefly employed to produce felted fabric from unspun wool. A buyer from Harrods, who attended the degree show, loved the hats and bought them. It would be quite a while before Dermott and I would think of ourselves as being 'in business', but this was the very first step.

building up the business

· · · · · · · · ·

There are probably as many ways of starting up a business as there are types of businesses, but it is fair to say that all of them require hard work, a steep learning curve and an element of luck. It also takes a degree of confidence to express your taste in your work, something that few people have when they are starting out, whether they are launching a new creative enterprise or finding their feet in their first job. Another aspect of it all that we soon discovered is that other people are not going to point you in the direction of the right supplier or producer, or share what amounts to their trade secrets: business is all about competition, and you have to find the information and contacts that you need yourself.

Our business, which has been a partnership from the beginning, is founded on teamwork. Dermott's background in project management in the construction industry and later his experience working in the financial department of a large company equipped him with just the sort of skills that any fledgling creative endeavour requires if the books are going to be balanced and growth is going to be steady and sustainable.

Every designer fears that their work will be overlooked, misunderstood or rejected, that their order books will be empty and that doors will fail to open for them. But in fact, success can be just as difficult to handle as a fear of failure, unless you have the right relationships in place with your suppliers and manufacturers and are able to depend on them completely. When the orders come in, whether they arrive in a flood or a trickle, you

Dermott and I outside our first studio in Battersea, London, in the mid-1990s.

33

Working on print boards and the layout of a lookbook.

orla kiely

accessories

ひとつひとつの商品を「永遠の名作」に…

Concept

色彩、生地、織物について卓越した知識を持つ オーラ カイリー。
実用性や品質にこだわりながら、それらの知識を生かし、モールスキンを他に
先駆けてバッグ素材に使うなど、常に新しい素材を心がける。

ひとつひとつの商品を「永遠の名作にしたい」という、ヨーロッパで注目されている
彼女のブランド「Orla Kiely」がついに日本でデビュー。

Profile

アイルランド出身である オーラ カイリーは、二人の祖母から受け継いだ
力強いビジネス センスと技巧を兼ね備えるデザイナー。

高校卒業後、ヨーロッパで最も古い芸術大学の一つである、
国立芸術デザイン大学（the National College of Art and Design ）
に進学し、プリント・テキスタイルを専攻。

在学中に、若いデザイナーに毎年贈られる、国際羊毛事務局賞（the International Wool Secretariat award ）を受賞。
その後、ロンドンの王立芸術学院（the Royal College of Art）に進み、修士号を取得。

'95年にバッグ ブランド「Orla Kiely」をスタートさせたほか、
「Paul Costelloe」、「Esprit」、「Habitat」、「Club Monaco」のデザインを担当した経験を持ち、
現在も「Marks and Spencer」のコンサルタントを務める。

Japanese booklet showing very early bag styles.

need to be certain that you can fulfil them by the deadlines you have agreed with your buyers and to the level of quality that is expected of you.

The response of the Harrods buyer had been encouraging, but even at the time it was clear that producing one-off designs was not the way forward. Dermott made the suggestion that we simplify matters somewhat, and so next season we produced cut-and-sew hats in a range of fresh and appealing colours that were made by a little factory that we had found. These were well-received, as were some fabric backpacks that I designed a little later.

Having built up our range a little more, there came what one might call a moment of insight. My father had come over from Ireland to visit our tiny stand at London Fashion Week where we were exhibiting. Looking around, he noticed that everyone there was carrying a bag, but very few of them were wearing hats. From that observation, everything changed and bags became the focus of our business.

When do you give up the day job? It depends. In my case, not for some time. For several years after leaving college I worked for a number of companies, both in London and abroad, including a year in Canada devising a children's range for Club Monaco, and a period as a consultant to the Marks and Spencer's design team. My weekends and spare time were devoted to designing what I wanted to produce myself. I was lucky: my superiors were supportive of what I was trying to do and the experience I gained was an invaluable way of building up confidence.

Design ideas are not enough. If these are going to be realized, you need suppliers you can trust and producers who share your vision and who will collaborate with you wholeheartedly. While I continued working, Dermott

Summer bags and hats featuring the Egg and Daisy spot print, spring 2000.

was busy sourcing factories and producers who might be prepared to work with us. Along the way, we had acquired an agent, and discovered Lineapelle, the huge trade fair in Bologna, Italy, where all the tanneries show.

It takes time to build up a base, and a good deal of planning and plotting. We found a proper handbag factory in Norwich, Norfolk, which did most of its work for Burberry, and after some persuasion, they agreed to work with us, as did another factory in Harpenden, Hertfordshire. Slowly we began to make a name for ourselves.

Dermott set up an office at home, managed the orders and deliveries, and succeeded in turning everything around so efficiently that the boxes of stock that the couriers delivered to our upstairs apartment during the day had been shipped out to our customers by the time I got back from work. It was a period of intense juggling, particularly as we had already started a family, but it was exciting to see things beginning to take shape.

The 'go for it' moment came at the end of 1997, when the British department store chain Debenhams asked me to launch a diffusion range for them as part of their Designers for Debenhams collection. As some of the other Designers for Debenhams included established names such as Lulu Guinness and Bill Amberg, it was a strong indication that we were on the right track. On the strength of this venture, and the degree of financial security that it offered, I finally gave up my job and devoted myself to designing for our label on a full-time basis.

Soon after that, we moved our office out of our home and into a business centre in nearby Battersea, south west London. It was a very basic building but full of friendly, creative people, all of whom were at the same stage of developing their businesses as we were.

Apples and Pears print bag and a very early Stem print on a classic shoulder bag.

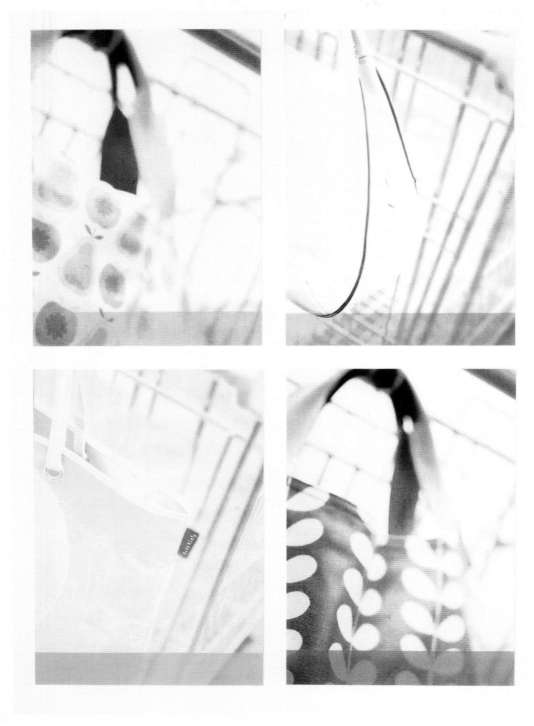

going into print

· · · · · · · · ·

By the end of the 1990s our bags and other accessories were increasingly well received, and we had grown in commercial expertise. Along with the small shops and scattered department stores that had been our first customers, we were starting to attract a larger and more international customer list, including Le Bon Marché in Paris, France, Isetan in Japan and Saks Fifth Avenue in New York, and we were showing our collections twice a year in Paris as well as in London.

During the 1990s accessories had tended to be rather sober and sombre. Black was big. Up to that point, our bag collections largely featured solid colours, and were generally made of fabric – suitings, coatings and tweeds – trimmed with leather. Occasionally, there might be the odd check or stripe bought in from a mill. Then everything changed when a friend of mine recommended a print factory to me, giving me the opportunity to develop my own patterns.

The factory that we found to produce our first printed-fabric accessories was smallish in scale, which meant that we were not obliged to buy fabric in bulk. Many larger producers impose what can be frightening 'minimums' for designers who are in the early stages of their careers, and instead of ordering, say, 10m (11 yards) of fabric to make your first samples, you have to undertake to buy 500m (547 yards), which can be a risk too far for a young business. Typically, a designer does a sample run, exhibits at a show and takes orders, promising delivery six months later. Committing

Early Stem print swatches with proposed constrast webbing handles.

Orla Kiely

yourself to buy a large 'minimum' of fabric ahead of firm customer orders – and with no track record – is a good way of losing money fast.

Judging by the reception we received for that first print collection, it was clear that people must have been hungry for colour and pattern again. Our stand at London Fashion Week, with its fresh, clear colours and punchy patterns, really stood out in a sea of monochrome. Although it was a couple of seasons later, when we introduced our Stem design, that the business took a quantum leap forward, we knew that we had found our signature look.

Stem, the pattern that has become our trademark and which to this day outsells everything else, dates from spring/summer 2001. The clean, flat look of the design owes something to my early preference for working in gouache. By the time Stem came out, we had progressed to computers to speed up the design process and the print began as a very quick drawing, which was then put straight onto screen for tweaking and refinement.

When we first introduced print, we produced a range of soft fabric bags in two patterns, one an oval egg design and the other a simple 1960s-style flower. The next year, we increased the weight of the cotton for more body, tweaked the styles and introduced Stem. We produced it in three colourways: olive and chartreuse, orange and ochre, and pink and red, with the graphic line that represented the stem always dark brown, providing a strong thread of consistency. By this time, people were beginning to get a taste for our patterns. While Stem was cute, it was not too pretty – it was clean, simple and strong, which was part of its appeal.

The original Stem design, with its white ground, was a summery print and we used it to make cotton canvas bags. Although the design did

Multi Stem has been a very popular pattern for bags, accessories and homeware.

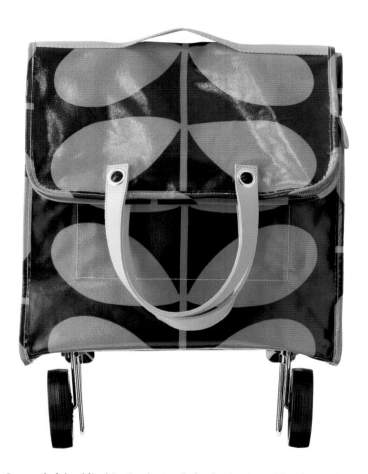

Canvas swatches for bags (left) and Giant Stem shopping trolley from the A/W 2008 Etc. diffusion bag range (above).

well, we decided not to include it in the following season's collection – cotton is not a fabric suitable for winter, when bags need to be made out of a more robust, weatherproof and structured material.

Nevertheless, it was when we were exhibiting our autumn/winter 2001 collection at London Fashion Week in spring of that year that I became convinced that pattern was missing. Then it dawned on me that if I recoloured Stem into darker tones and had the cloth laminated to make it stronger, more durable and easy to wipe clean, we could include the print in the winter range. Such a simple, logical step, and no one was doing anything like it at the time – laminated fabric, in those days, meant tablecloths.

When I dashed back to the studio to make rough colour sketches, I had no idea whether our factory had the facilities to laminate fabric, or whether the print in the new colours could be produced fast enough to be included in the forthcoming show in Paris. All I knew for certain when I faxed the sketches through was that the factory still had the screens from the previous season. Two weeks later, by some miracle, they had turned it all around. By the time we exhibited the collection at Première Classe, we had the new Stem bags in the winter colourways of brown and cream, dark khaki and olive, Bordeaux and pink. As I had suspected, the lamination had given the fabric more structure, so the bags held their shape better.

Première Classe is one of the world's leading accessories shows and takes place during Paris Fashion Week. The first inkling we had that the print was going to be a huge success came when hordes of Japanese buyers suddenly descended on our stall. One of our co-exhibitors, who had the neighbouring stand, said it was like a JAL 747 had just landed in the Jardin du Luxembourg and all the passengers had disembarked

Wool Tapestry Stem handbag from A/W 2008 mainline bag collection.

and come straight to us. Once the collection reached the shops, the print sold incredibly well, exceeding all of our expectations.

Since then, every collection has always featured a variation of Stem. One season we produced the print in very dark colours – grey, dark blue and brown, all with black stems. Initial feedback from the buyers suggested that they wouldn't be as popular, because people wanted and expected colour from us, but in fact they flew off the shelves. Over the years, Stem has appeared on a range of products, from bags to wallets, from mugs to wallpaper. Every new season we modify and recolour it. It's been used as a linear or outline print; it's been embossed to make a textural pattern; and it's appeared in multiple colours. In 2009 a soft, layered version of the design – Butterfly Stem – appears on a bag specially designed for Maggie's, the cancer charity.

Nearly a decade since the launch of Stem and our business has grown out of all recognition from those early days. From that first room in the Battersea business centre, we gradually, almost organically, expanded until we had taken over two, three, and then four units, along with a stockroom. Once we were a little larger, we were able to establish a central warehouse and distribution centre to process our increasing volume of orders fast and efficiently.

Now we have our own dedicated design studio and office in Clapham, south west London, on three floors of a light, airy purpose-built building, where our staff of designers and production team work amid rails of samples, presentation boards and props for forthcoming shows. Visitors might share the reception area with vintage coffee tables sourced on eBay, or a large mock-up of a 1950s television set for screening the latest collection. Since every day is 'Take Your Dog to Work Day', they may also be greeted by Olive, the office dog.

A postcard created for Japanese shops showing Flower Stem bags and accessories (S/S 2004).

ORLA KIELY

LONDON

fun, cheerful and bursting with colour...
brighten up someone's christmas
with a special gift from orla kiely

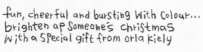

+ Link

Orla Kiely

Belt Loops
Orla
Scavato

Frames
Giglio

A2B

SUPERGLASS
Reversible

RANCH +
PATENT

PATENT

BIG PLASTIC
BUCKLE

FRAMES TO.
COVER - CLIC

stitched
seem

PLASTIC
BUCKLES
CREAM.
PATCHWORK

?

Mavi

MAVI   A12

PADMACH

MAVI

MILAGROS/

PADPA

We all work as a team. Production, Sales and Marketing are based on the ground floor, while on the top floor Dermott controls and manages the increasingly complex business side, from Accounts and Logistics to Strategic Planning. The design area where I spend most of my time is on the second floor, where the light is best. It's often hectic and bustling, but the informality of the open layout suits the collaborative nature of the way we work.

Back when we first introduced print, our collections were tiny and were chiefly focused on bags. After Stem, we began to add a small amount of clothing to the range and as it grew we took on an American agent. Now we produce a full collection of womenswear, both mainline and diffusion; bags and accessories; home furnishings for the bedroom, bathroom, kitchen and living areas; as well as luggage, stationery and umbrellas. Our products and ranges are sold in countries all over the world and in hundreds of outlets, from specialist shops to department stores. Our flagship store in London's Covent Garden opened in 2005, followed by stores in Tokyo, Paris and Hong Kong, while our website provides a virtual and ever-changing shop window.

Somewhere along the way a successful business becomes a brand, a designer's name becomes a label. There comes a moment when you are suddenly aware just how many times you have seen someone at a supermarket checkout pull out a wallet that you have designed. Or you open a magazine to see a celebrity photographed wearing your clothes. Becoming a brand is not simply a function of size or exposure, although both come into it. Far more important is quality and control, developing a design language that is both immediately recognizable and able to evolve in fresh new directions.

Previous pages: A working notebook showing swatches and Pantone colour references.

Multi Stem on a tram in Hong Kong promoting the brand.

Our flagship store in Monmouth Street, Covent Garden opened in 2005.

Monmouth Street shop interior, spring/summer, 2010.

2
inspiration

inspiration

· · · · · · · · ·

Where do ideas come from? It's a question that many designers find hard to answer. Sometimes there is an obvious and direct connection between a specific source and a design concept. At other times, the whole process is less clear-cut, and an idea may arise instead from a mysterious cross-fertilization of various images that you have tucked away in your memory over the years.

Developing a creative eye means first of all learning to look. It means discovering what you like, what shapes, colours, moods and themes say most to you and spark your imagination. In a sense, it is also a question of developing confidence in your own preferences so that you can make visual and critical judgments. In other words, so that you can edit and select.

Many art students nowadays are encouraged to keep sketchbooks in which they are asked to note ideas, colours, patterns and references to other types of visual material as they go along. This is as much about learning how to look – or how to pay attention – as it is about creating a resource of imagery that might suggest various avenues of exploration to be fruitfully pursued at a later date. Like most designers, I am an avid collector of books and other sources of reference that may directly or indirectly inspire themes for print collections or photo shoots. I find it very hard to throw anything away. You never know when it might be useful.

Inspiration is always the beginning of the design process. Next comes the research phase, where you delve into it all in more detail, gathering information of various kinds and trying out ideas in sketches and drawings.

Previous pages: Close-up of bookshelves in my studio.

You don't have to be a student of art or design to benefit from the same type of discipline. It is all too easy to catch a fleeting sight of an image or scene that appeals to you and then forget it further down the line when you might want to refer to it. Keeping a scrapbook or a digital file of images helps with any kind of creative decision-making, whether you are choosing colours for your home or putting together a wardrobe. With the internet offering a visual treasure-trove at your fingertips and most cellphones now including a good camera, building up your own personal image bank has never been easier.

When you make your living in design, as I do, you never stop absorbing ideas from the world around you, even if you aren't consciously aware of it at the time. It can be the smallest thing – products on a supermarket shelf, wild flowers in a park, a knife and fork. It's all about taking mental snapshots of everyday things, mundane or random, old or new.

Building up a frame of visual reference takes time. The key factor is to expose yourself to as much as possible, to keep looking and thinking. Exhibitions of artists' work and textile collections have an obvious bearing on graphic or design work. In a broader sense, inspiration can also come from travel and other cultures, from urban or rural landscapes, from other media, such as film or television, and from the past.

On our very first trip to Japan, we were invited to spend a weekend at one of the best-known traditional guesthouses, or *ryokan*, in Kyoto, the

Tawaraya. The Japanese concept of hospitality is that each person (or couple) should feel as if they were subject to the unique attentions of their hosts, and great care was taken to ensure that none of the guests crossed paths with one another. What has remained with me ever since, however, was the attention to detail, the tiny wooden toggles that served as closures on the doors, and the way that all the technology in the room – the television and the phone – were covered in vegetable-dyed linen.

My own sources of inspiration are naturally quite subjective, just as anyone's would be and should be. They include mid-century modern design, particularly Scandinavian modern, various artists and designers, especially those whose work has a strong graphic element, and all things vintage and retro.

An oversized vintage-look TV made for London Fashion Week, showcasing our S/S 2010 film.

These snapshots were taken on a research trip to Tokyo. Overleaf: Mid-century modern is a particular source of inspiration.

art & film

· · · · · · · · · ·

It is perhaps not surprising that many of the artists who have most inspired me are those who have produced work with a strong graphic element: Fernand Léger, with his use of bold primaries and geometric forms, for example, and Henri Matisse, particularly his late collages or 'cut-outs', such as *La Tristesse du Roi* (1952) and the famous *The Snail* (1953), to name but two. The avant-garde Russian artist Lyubov Popova and the Constructivist Varvara Stepanova were other artists who had an immense effect on me, particularly when I was a student.

Most fashion or print designers will cite Sonia Delaunay as an early influence and when I was a student I was no exception. Delaunay, who was a painter and textile designer and who also designed stage sets for the theatre, was influenced by Cubism. She was supposedly inspired to use geometric forms and primary colour in her work, which had previously been more representational and naturalistic, after making a quilted blanket for her newborn son and appreciating the vibrant effect of the juxtaposed colours and shapes.

When I first went to New York, the work of graffiti artist Keith Haring caught my eye, as well as the work of Jean-Michel Basquiat. But that was the 1980s. More recently, a few of us from the studio went to visit the wonderful Louisiana Museum of Modern Art outside Copenhagen. At that time the museum was mounting an exhibition of the work of Danish landscape artist Per Kirkeby. The painterly contrast of colour in his canvases enthralled me and was one of the inspirations behind the colour palette for our autumn/winter 2009 collection.

Paintings by Guiseppe Gambino from the 1960s. An artist I discovered on a trip to Italy.

69

Just as visiting galleries and museums can provide fruitful ideas for how to combine colours and how to put shapes together in balanced yet lively compositions, film can also suggest ideas for both design and styling. Sometimes these will be more amorphous – perhaps simply taking the form of a mood or theme – while at other times you may be more specifically inspired by the cut, line and silhouette of clothing or costume. The variations on a 1960s look, as shown by Audrey Hepburn in *Breakfast at Tiffany's*, Mia Farrow in *Rosemary's Baby*, Catherine Deneuve in *Belle de Jour*, and similar cinematic classics of the period, have been a constant source of interest and inspiration.

As a teenager, one of my favourite treats on a typically Irish rainy Saturday afternoon was to watch matinée films on television. I loved films from the 1940s, 1950s and 1960s, lapping up the style of stars such as Bette Davis, Katharine Hepburn and Grace Kelly. I remember seeing *The Fountainhead* (dir. King Vidor, 1949) with Gary Cooper and Patricia Neal, and being wowed by the creative vision and integrity of the main character. I also enjoyed classic British films. Kitchen-sink dramas, such as *Room at the Top* (dir. Jack Clayton, 1959) and *A Taste of Honey* (dir. Tony Richardson, 1961), and other 1960s films, such as *Darling* (dir. John Schlesinger, 1965).

I am also a fan of French cinema from this period. Recently, I have been revisiting some old favourites, notably *Les parapluies de Cherbourg* (dir. Jacques Demy, 1964) and *Les demoiselles de Rochefort* (dir. Jacques Demy and Agnès Varda, 1967). The mood, colour, style, storyline and music of *Les demoiselles* together created a film that is still fresh and inspiring – a visual treat. Obviously, when I was a teenager and seeing such films for the first time, I wasn't deliberately setting out to take note of those things, but somehow they have stayed with me all the same.

Marcello Mastroianni and Sophia Loren in 'La Moglie del Prete' ('The Priest's Wife'), 1970.

vintage & mid-century modern

· · · · · · · · · ·

Although making a distinction between mid-century modern and vintage or retro may seem like splitting hairs, retro is perhaps more about the type of anonymous furniture, clothing, textiles and bric-a-brac that you might find on a market stall than it is about the more famous pieces that have a traceable and identifiable pedigree, such as an Eero Saarinen 'Tulip' chair or an Alvar Aalto stool. Many mid-century modern designs are viewed as contemporary classics, and rightfully so. Vintage pieces are often mass-market interpretations of a similar aesthetic or style, and have a quirky charm and a certain cosiness that is very appealing.

When I was growing up, Dublin was not a great place for markets. There was one in the town hall, but you really had to rummage to find anything worth having. It was when I first went to New York and, later, when I was working at Esprit and was travelling a good deal, that I really became enamoured of vintage style, especially designs from the 1960s and 1970s. New York's thrift shops and vintage stores were eye-openers. So, too, was Porte de Montreuil, one of Paris's many markets. Unlike the better-known Porte de Clignancourt, which nowadays is quite expensive, Montreuil is a proper flea market, with a jumble of second-hand clothes and bits and bobs in among the car parts, used appliances and other detritus. It is a real treasure-trove for anyone interested in retro style, particularly vintage clothing. London has no shortage of great markets, either, from the frenetic bustle of Portobello Road and Camden Lock to vibrant Greenwich Market. There are also many

A selection of some of the vintage fabrics I have collected (right). Previous pages: Mood board for S/S 2009 collection.

AN EXCLUSIVE *Schumacher*

second-hand shops on Brick Lane and wonderful junk shops, salvage yards and other second-hand outlets scattered around from borough to borough.

Like most twenty-somethings, my early forays into flea markets and thrift shops were chiefly for the purpose of buying clothes to wear – printed knitted sweaters, skirts, dresses and those big men's jackets that were so fashionable in the 1980s. Nowadays, I am more likely to buy furniture or objects for our home, or to serve as props in fashion shoots and shows, although eBay is increasingly providing a quick and easy source of vintage pieces.

Bargains aside, browsing through market stalls or in a charity shop is a good exercise for any designer. Because presentation isn't generally a key consideration, you have to develop a keen eye to find the treasures among the less desirable items. At the same time, the fact that often prices are rock bottom means that your choice or selection is not biased by the perceived value that a high price tag confers. Instead, you have to learn to trust your taste and your judgment – to feel the fabric to gauge its quality, or to examine the way a table is constructed. Most importantly, markets are great sources of reference material for colour ideas, patterns, silhouette and line.

As a designer, I have always believed that functionality is king, which made me a natural convert to modernism in my twenties and has given me a special affection for the mid-century version of it. After the pioneers of the early modern movement brought functionalism to the fore in design and architecture in the early decades of the twentieth century, the next great phase of contemporary design occurred after the Second World War, when Scandinavian modern designers first found widespread international recognition. The first wave of modernism focused on machine forms and materials – furniture made of metal tubing, for example. The second phase was warmer and more human in its appeal. Much of that approachability was down to the Scandinavian preference for wood, teak and bent plywood, in particular, and to a broader and more cheerful colour palette.

While no less clean-lined than early modernist work, mid-century designs typically display curves and organic forms, and as a consequence are less uncompromising and easier to live with, which helped them find a mass-market audience in the 1950s and 1960s. Those who could afford it bought original designs by great contemporary designers such as Hans Wegner, Finn Juhl, Arne Jacobsen and Charles and Ray Eames; others sought out more affordable furniture and fittings produced by manufacturers such as the British company Ercol, whose designs shared a similar aesthetic. Other outstanding contemporary mass-market designs were those produced for the British manufacturer Stag by John and Sylvia Reid. Not as well known today as Ercol furniture, the Stag ranges were hugely popular in the late 1950s and early 1960s, and helped to bring the sleek, modern look into greater prominence.

My first exposure to Scandinavian, in particular Danish, design was through the products stocked by Dublin's innovative Stock Shop, which carried a range of homewares and print designs. What I especially appreciated was the sense of optimism such designs conveyed. Later, I became familiar with many of the other great designers of the period and over the years I have built up a reference library of their work, which has been a constant source of ideas.

I was able to draw on such sources when we were invited to collaborate with the British retailer Heal's, who have long been at the forefront of contemporary design. Our furniture range for Heal's, launched in 2008, captures a flavour of that exciting and forward-looking time mixed with a twenty-first century aesthetic.

One important area where contemporary style reigned supreme across the board in the late 1940s, 1950s and early 1960s was in pattern design. After the war, new designers emerged with new themes to pursue, and the textiles and wallpapers they produced represented a complete break with the past, a real breath of fresh air. It was a fruitful period of collaboration and cross-fertilization, with many artists designing prints for fabric and papers. In the late 1940s, for example, dress fabrics and scarf designs commissioned by the London-based company, Ascher Ltd, featured prints by Jean Cocteau, Barbara Hepworth, Henry Moore and Lucian Freud, among other artists. At the same time, many textile designers took their cue directly from the work of contemporary artists such as Jackson Pollock, Alexander Calder, Paul Klee and Joan Miró.

Out went traditional florals, sprigged prints and naturalistic renderings of leaves and in came designs inspired not only by contemporary art but also by architectural forms and new scientific discoveries. Nature was still an important element, but focus fell on the structure, skeleton or silhouette of growth, on the whole plant, not simply the flower. There was a loose, freehand feeling to many of these 'Contemporary' designs, with blots, doodles, smudges and hatching giving both a tactile quality and a sense of energy and vitality. A particular point of reference was the new art form of the mobile, especially in the way motifs were arranged across the ground as if suspended in space.

The British textile designer Lucienne Day (1917–2010) was responsible for a huge body of work and her patterns remain striking and original to this day. Like her husband Robin (1915–2010), the famous furniture designer, she believed that modern design could make the world a better place, banishing the dreariness of the war years and the period of austerity that followed. The paintings of Klee and Miró, along with the sculptures of

Rowan table and chairs, part of our furniture range for Heal's.

Naum Gabo and Alexander Calder's mobiles, were direct inspirations. Calyx, her linear print depicting spidery plant forms, was first displayed at the Festival of Britain in 1951 and went on to attract international acclaim. Many more followed. Over a period of 20 years, she produced 70 patterns for Heal's, along with designs for other textile, wallpaper and ceramics companies. On pattern design, she said: 'It is not enough to "choose a motif", nor enough to "have ideas" and be able to draw. There must also be the ability to weld the single units into a homogenous whole, so that the pattern seems to be part of the cloth.' This she was able to achieve incredibly well.

Textural effect was also an overriding concern during the period. In the early 1950s Hungarian textile designer Tibor Reich (1916–96) produced a range of screen-printed designs that he called 'textureprints'. These made use of close-up photographs of natural textures, such as bark or straw, which emphasized the woven nature of the textile.

Another source of reference was architecture. During the 1950s Swedish textile designer Astrid Sampe (1909–2002) produced designs for the progressive American furniture company Knoll, including Lazy Lines, a spare, striped pattern inspired by modern architecture. Until Knoll commissioned a number of designers to produce exclusive prints, they had been unable to source suitable furnishing fabric for their contemporary furniture ranges and had been using suiting from British tailors.

The Swedish designer Stig Lindberg (1916–82) also produced work for Knoll. While much Scandinavian pattern design was abstract, minimal and textural, his early prints, Pottery and Lustgården, both of which he created for an exhibition curated by Astrid Sampe in 1947, are colourful, pictorial and show the obvious influence of folk art.

Herman Miller was another American furniture manufacturer to introduce textile production in the 1950s. The department was headed by Alexander Girard, whose own designs, although abstract, simple and based around a limited range of motifs, achieved great depth through overlapping and through an inspired use of colour.

Developments in screen-printing made larger-scale motifs increasingly possible. Toward the end of the period, bold graphic prints, such as those designed by Maija Isola (1927–2001) for the Finnish textile company Marimekko came to the fore. By the 1960s Pop Art and Op Art were beginning to have an impact on print design, followed by a more eclectic mix in the late 1960s and early 1970s.

Maija Islola, like Lucienne Day and Sonia Delaunay, is often cited as an inspiration for designers who work with pattern. Less well known, but to me even more important, was the British textile designer Barbara Brown, especially the work she did for Heal's Fabrics in the late 1960s and 1970s. Barbara Brown began designing textiles in the 1950s; by the early 1960s her designs had become much larger in scale and often geometric in theme, such as Reciprocation (1962), a pattern comprised of circles and squares. The influence of Op Art can be seen in Expansion (1966) or the eye-watering Spiral (1969). Bold and often architectural, many of her patterns, such as the swirling Frequency (1969), also show an incredibly subtle and rich use of colour. They don't date at all.

While I have a particular nostalgic affection for the patterns of the 1960s and 1970s, what is so striking about the 'Contemporary' or mid-modern period is the sheer quality and inventiveness that was expressed in print. Such designs, with their optimism and spontaneity, are an invaluable resource for anyone interested in pattern.

Overleaf: The textures and mark-making displayed by vintage textiles are a great source of inspiration.

1 2

3 4

5 6

1 *Impromptu* free-form abstract hand-print on linen or cotton in celadon/blue/lavender/black. By Laverne Inc. USA
2 *Ravenna* screen-print on crash in five colourways including scarlet/chocolate, light and dark green, royal blue/black. Designed by Mary Oliver, MSIA, for Donald Bros Ltd UK
3 *Sumac* textured leaf pattern hand-screen-print in a wide range of colourings on linen, fibreglass and Fortisan fabrics. By Elenhank Designers Inc. USA

4 *Rivoli* hand-screen-print in 'landscape colours' on 'Cretonne Riviera'. Designed by H. Schmidt GERMANY for Manifattura JSA, ITALY
5 *Bari* machine-print on Rosebank cretonne, with white linear pattern on a blurred ground of bright and subdued colourings. Designed by Simbari ITALY for Turnbull & Stockdale Ltd UK
6 *Sweet Briar* machine-print on cotton in five colourways. Designed by Barbara Brown for Heal's of London UK

7 *Cables* hand-screen-print in a wide choice of colours on natural 'Angelstripe' linen; repeat 31 inches. By Adler-Schnee Associates USA

8 *Kamm* hand-block-print in black on fine white cotton. By Elisabeth Burri-Anliker Textilentwerferin, SWB, SWITZERLAND

9 *Legions* screen-printed cotton in three-colour combinations: yellows, blues, violet/greys or brown/greys. Designed by Cliff Holden for Hull Traders Ltd UK

10 *Hexagon* machine-print on cotton in 4 colourways. Designed by Dorothy Smith for Morton Sundour Fabrics Ltd UK

11 *Cotil 5812* two-colour cotton print in blue, yellow, and green tones and in yellow/green. Designed by Mette Lac for A/S C. Olesen DENMARK

12 *Aurora* brush-stroke screen-print in blues, browns, oranges and greens with black, on strong cotton. Designed by Cliff Holden for Edinburgh Weavers UK

13, 14 *Blossoming Trees* cotton screen-print in black on white, by Aleksandra Lewińska; and *Hens* two-colour print in yellow and black on white cotton, by Alicja Gutkowska: The Warsaw Institute of Industrial Design POLAND

colour

colour

• • • • • • • • •

Colour is an incredibly powerful element in design, as it is in life. A short cut to the emotions, it is almost visceral in the way it connects with our moods and feelings. A poppy-red scarf wrapped around your neck on a grey November morning warms your spirits as surely as it keeps out the cold. Painting the walls an edgy shade of grey-green creates an intimate and cosy mood against which brighter accents of yellow and orange sing with added intensity. Colour is happy, sexy and playful. It feeds the soul.

Despite the widespread availability of colour in every area of life, from clothing to wallpaper and paint, from bed linen to pots and pans, many people fight shy of it. While fashions in clothing and interiors do go through their periodic patches of monochrome – 'black is the new black' – there are those who remain ill at ease with colour regardless of what is in the shops or featured on the pages of a glossy magazine. Perhaps this is because they are daunted by the sheer choice of colours available and fear that they might get it 'wrong', or perhaps they are simply uncertain how to handle its emotional power, or worry about standing out from the crowd and calling attention to themselves. All of which might account for the rather depressing popularity of 'magnolia' as a safe wall colour. Whichever is the case, life without colour is not merely cooking without seasoning, it's cooking without half the ingredients.

I always keep an eye open and love to find images that inspire my colour sense and make me smile. The picture of the building with brightly dressed models standing in the windows is one of my favourites. The photographer

Previous pages: Storyboard for our website featuring A/W 2009 ad campaign images.

'Girls in the Windows' (1960) by Ormond Gigli.

came across the building, which was derelict and due to be demolished the next day, and quickly organized the shoot – that would never be allowed today. Another image that I came across when I was a student really inspired me then and still does. On the road to Thoiry (1970) was taken by the Swiss photographer Peter Knapp (b.1931) for the French fashion house Courrèges. The empty road and open landscape evoke a feeling of youthfulness and adventure, while the two graphic spots of colour – the space-hopper and the bright orange Renault 4 van – are playful and nostalgic at the same time. There's so much carefree energy in this picture – it seems to say that anything is possible. For me, what it also taps into are childhood memories of summer holidays.

Like pattern, colour almost disappeared from our homes during the 1990s, except, perhaps, in the form of stranded accents introduced rather self-consciously in spare, muted backgrounds, where they seemed to be making some sort of apology for themselves. This was a time when neutral, natural or monochrome palettes reigned supreme in the form of pure white walls, pale hardwood or stone floors, glass and stainless steel. In fashion, too, colour was largely absent or used in solid blocks unrelieved by accent or pattern. Advocates of minimalism attest to its spirituality and serenity, but for those of us who enjoy colour, such blank canvases amount to sensory deprivation.

Now colour is back in the mainstream of taste and people are rediscovering the added dimension it brings to life, its irrepressible cheerfulness and vitality, the brave face it puts on for the world. Rather than a paintbox of primary shades or tentative, hesitant pastels, strong evocative colours that hover on the edge of one colour and the next – olive, ochre, aubergine, burnt orange, acid yellow, mouse brown – have come to the fore, partnered in delicious, irresistible combinations.

One of my favourite images: 'On the road to Thoiry' (1970) by Peter Knapp for Courrèges.

91

Colour is vital to me. I can't work or live without colour around me and it is central to what I do. For me, it is where the process of design begins.

Today we take it for granted that colour is infinitely varied, affordable and everywhere – the epitome of cheap and cheerful. Yet technological advances in printing and reproduction, in paints and dyes and in visual communications of all forms, mean that we live in a much more colourful world than ever before.

Our world is not only more colourful than it was in the past, but we also encounter much more visual stimulus in our daily lives, not simply through mass media, such as the internet, television and film, but also through the ease with which we can travel to far-flung corners of the globe, an exposure that has opened our eyes to the vital role colour plays in different cultures. Only half a century or so ago, unless you were very well-heeled or exceptionally adventurous, you would have to rely on second-hand descriptions or poor-quality reproductions of those vibrant colour combinations that today every gap-year traveller can see for themselves: the ice-cream colours of the Caribbean, the vibrant pinks and reds of Rajasthan, the hot and spicy palette of Central America, or the free-for-all of Holi, the Hindu spring festival, where people pelt each other with coloured powder and coloured water. Such exuberant examples of a delight in colour for its own sake cannot fail to have an impact on a home-grown colour sense.

Although people have always tried to surround themselves with colour, the vibrant colours found in nature were difficult to reproduce until modern times. Until the nineteenth century the range of colours available for practical use was extremely limited by today's standards. Up until this time, paints and pigments were exclusively derived from natural sources – animal, vegetable or

Raincoats, bags and hats in primary colours from the A/W 2004 collection.

mineral – and bright, strong shades were expensive and rare. Bright yellow was unknown until the invention of chrome yellow in the early nineteenth century. This is not to say that in the past everyone wore drab clothing or lived in drab surroundings – historical dress and interior schemes can be surprisingly vivid and rich, and a fruitful source of reference in themselves – but historically colour was more often the preserve of the better-off. Sumptuary laws, enacted in many centuries and cultures, often underscored the exclusiveness of certain shades.

Advances in synthetic pigments at the turn of the nineteenth century, followed by the invention of chemical, or aniline, dyes in the middle of it, broadened the palette considerably and produced colours of greater intensity. But even with these advances, it was not until developments in the petrochemical industry after the Second World War that colour really began to permeate everyday life, almost to saturation point. While it may take a programme such as *The Thirties in Colour*, with its previously unseen colour documentary footage, to remind us that life prewar was not conducted in black and white, colour was nevertheless nowhere near as prevalent as it is today.

In the late 1930s, when cinematographers, costume designers and set designers were working on *The Wizard of Oz*, colour was still a spectacle. As we watch Dorothy transported by a tornado from black-and-white Kansas to the vibrantly hued, rainbow world of the Land of Oz, we can gain some idea of the impact of the arrival of colour in cinema. *The Wizard of Oz* was in part conceived as an advertisement for Technicolor, at a time when films were black and white, few books had colour plates and coloured postcards were largely hand-tinted. From Dorothy's ruby slippers to the green horses in the Emerald City, colour could burst out of the screen and wow an audience with the sheer novelty of it all. One of the interesting challenges for today's designers,

Leather Stitched Stem bag in orange, A/W 2008.

now that the colour palette has broadened to encompass all manner of shades, and nuances of shades, from neon to fluorescent, is to find a way of recapturing that same sense of wonder, to make colour fresh and exciting again.

As a source of colour, nature is second to none. You only have to stare into the depths of a tropical fish tank or watch a wildlife programme on the television to appreciate that the natural world is a place of vivid intensity and startling colour combinations. Nature is greedy for colour.

A walk in the park during autumn exposes you to the moody contrast of orange and yellow leaves drifting down against grey misty skies. A stroll along the beach gives you time to appreciate the infinite subtlety of the many shades of blue where the sea meets the sky. A rolling field of acid-yellow rapeseed, the scarlet stains of poppies in the verges, the graphic flash of a magpie's wings, are all reminders that there is nothing reticent or retiring about nature's colour palette and pattern book.

Nature is not only a source of colour ideas, for many centuries it was the only means to make colour. Blue was derived from the plant sources indigo and woad. Red was made from madder, another plant, or from cochineal and kermes, both insect dyes. Weld, the bark of the American black oak, broom, heather, birch and poplar twigs were all used to make yellow. These basic dyes in various combinations were the means of making black, green, purple and orange.

When the new chemical dyes became available in the mid-nineteenth century, some complained that they were garish and lacked the softness and subtleties of the old vegetable-based colours. Designers such as William Morris (1834–96) went to great lengths to preserve those traditional dyeing skills and knowledge. At Morris's works at Merton Abbey, a favourite spectacle for visitors was seeing sea-green skeins of wool emerge from the indigo dyeing vat, magically transforming a few minutes later into a deep, dusky blue on exposure to the air.

Today, organic or natural sources of colour still have a role to play, particularly as environmental awareness comes to the fore. While, for the sake of convenience, most people generally prefer their clothing and furnishing textiles to be dyefast, there is something deeply appealing about fabrics that gently fade with each wash, until they become as comfortable and familiar as a second skin. When natural or vegetable colours fade, they do so with a certain softness and in balance with one another, so that colour relationships are preserved. Natural dyes often have great depth of character, too. Leather that has been coloured with vegetable dyes, for example, has a degree of depth and richness that is lacking when the dyes are synthetic.

Throughout history, from the first handprints on the walls of caves, all artists have been intimately concerned with colour – with the arcane processes and sources of making different pigments, with colour's layers of meaning and association, and with the relationship of colour to light. Like colour names derived from nature, such as leaf green, artist's colours, such as viridian and vermilion, are also very evocative, not least because they are so exact.

Looking at the work of those artists who were particularly obsessed with colour is a great source of inspiration. The poised balance of primary shades in Piet Mondrian's work, for example, the intense blue-greens of Henri Matisse or the luminous colour combinations and graduations of Patrick Heron's paintings saturate your eyes with colour and heighten your awareness. For such artists, the use of colour was often instinctive. 'My choice of colour does not rely on any scientific theory; it is based on observation, on feeling, on the very nature of each experience,' said Matisse.

Vincent van Gogh was an artist who was particularly interested in the relationship of complementary colours. His letters to his brother Theo express an acute degree of observation and sensitivity to colour. To take but one example, in this extract from a letter written on 31 July 1888 he is describing a coal boat moored at a quay on the Rhone: 'Seen from above it was all glistening and wet from a shower; the water was a white yellow and clouded pearl-grey, the sky lilac and an orange strip in the west, the town violet. On the boat, small workmen, blue and dirty white, were coming and going.' 'White yellow' and 'dirty white' – those descriptions are so precise. And we can see just how reverberant an orange strip would appear against a lilac sky, and visualize in exactly which proportions those colours would have to be.

Less difficult to categorize, perhaps, are what you might call sources of 'found' colour – fortuitous combinations or particular shades that you happen upon. A fairground sign, a bag of boiled sweets, a particularly electric partnering of colours displayed on packaging or printed on a can, a stack of multicoloured Fiestaware on a vintage stall, a peeling poster in an alleyway, an old Polaroid snapshot may seem mundane in comparison to the work of great artists, but they can be just as stimulating and valuable for colour ideas. With most cellphones featuring digital cameras of considerable technological sophistication, such moments need pass no one by.

When we are scouting locations for our fashion shoots, the 'found' colours in a particular setting can be an extremely important part of the whole visual story, reinforcing or complementing our palette for a particular season. A great location we discovered one season was an old café where the banquettes were upholstered in red, ochre and olive, an ideal backdrop to the collection we were presenting.

Retro cafés provided the locations for the A/W 2007 photoshoot. Overleaf: Café in Eastbourne.

colour families

· · · · · · · · ·

When it comes to working with colour, experience and experiment count for much more than theory or analysis. In fact, theory can inhibit creativity, as can those old-fashioned adages about which colours 'clash' and should never be seen together – as our grandmothers might have cautioned against the combination of red and pink, for example, or blue and green. You will find many colour clashes in nature, but none that are uncomfortable or jarring. In the end, colour is all about feeling and response.

Colour is a function of the way our eyes see light. As Sir Isaac Newton was the first to discover, when white light strikes a prism, it breaks up into bands of colour. Each colour corresponds to a different wavelength of radiant energy, which is depicted as the familiar rainbow spectrum of red, orange, yellow, green, blue and violet. In reality, the spectrum is not made of distinct bands, but is continuous, from the longest wavelengths, which are red, to the shortest, which are violet, and extending in either direction to infrared and ultraviolet, which our eyes are not equipped to see. The reason why an apple appears to be red is because it has absorbed all the wavelengths of light, except those that correspond to red, which are reflected back to our eyes.

The science of colour helps to explain our emotional responses to different shades. Colours from the 'warm' end of the spectrum – reds, oranges and yellows – are said to be 'advancing', which means they leap out at you and catch your eye. Reds and oranges put us on alert because they correspond to the longer wavelengths of light and our eyes have to make

Illustration from a catalogue for London Fashion Week showing our spinaker holdall.

the maximum adjustment to see them. When you see red, your pulse rate literally increases. That physical effort translates into a feeling of stimulus.

Colours from the 'cool' end of the spectrum – blues, greys and violets – which correspond to the shorter wavelengths, are soothing and 'distancing'. The blue of the horizon or the haziness of distant mountains encapsulates that quality of airiness and spaciousness.

Bang in the middle are various shades of green. Because green occupies the middle of the spectrum, our eyes don't have to adjust very much to see it, which makes it a supremely restful and easy-going colour, whether it is the green of a landscape or the green of an awning shading a window from strong light. When light levels fall at the end of the day, the middle of the spectrum shifts slightly toward blue; 'l'heure bleue' is the evocative French term for twilight.

What you won't find in the spectrum or in various theoretical models, such the colour wheel, are those natural and neutral shades of black, white, grey, brown, cream, beige and so on, colours that are very useful in design and pattern creation, not only for creating graphic interest or introducing breathing space, but also for their inherent subtleties. Brown is a colour that shows the greatest degree of variation, which is not surprising as it is achieved by mixing more than two colours together. It can be reddish, blackish, greyish, yellowish – echoing the vast and evocative range of browns in nature itself.

Through associations, from the personal to the cultural, different meanings also come into play when we think about or react to colour. In the West, for example, women traditionally marry in white and black is the colour of mourning, while in many Asian countries, people mourn in white and marry in red. We see pink as naturally feminine, yet as fashion icon Diana Vreeland (1903–89) famously stated: 'Pink is the navy blue of India.' Yellow is the colour of long life in China. Green is variously the colour of jealousy, envy, nature and fertility; while red spells danger, love, passion and fire. Added to these cultural associations, there are personal ways in which different people respond to certain colours, which may be embedded in childhood memories, all of which affect the way colours are individually perceived. My own colour preferences are indelibly linked to the colours I remember seeing all around me when I was growing up – the oranges, browns and greens of a 1960s palette.

Then there are what you might call received notions, such as how to apply colour remedially to improve the quality of natural light in an interior, for example, or how to use colour to make the most of spatial limitations. Sometimes such rules of thumb can be helpful, but often they simply serve as a reminder that rules are there to be broken.

The truth is that when it comes to using and choosing colour there is no real substitute for practice. Handling colour successfully is all about looking and developing your eye, trying different combinations, mixing shades until you arrive at the one you want, collecting swatches and samples. One way of broadening your colour horizons is to keep a digital folder or scrapbook of colour ideas – pictures torn out of magazines, postcards, scraps of fabric, packaging, or images downloaded from blogs and websites – anything that catches your eye. With practice you can train your eye to make ever more precise distinctions, and precision is what the successful use of colour is all about. Above all, it is most important to be guided by what speaks to you. Using colour is all about expressing yourself.

The scores of names we have for different colours give an inkling of the infinite and subtle variety from one shade to the next. Take blue, for example. Is it navy, indigo, ink, sky, petrol, teal, azure, cobalt, royal, sea,

Overleaf: Sketchbook pages showing a working colour chart, alongside David Bailey's photo of Grace Coddington.

Orla Kiely

PANTONE®
302 M

PANTONE®
7489 C

PANTONE®
5503 C

PANTONE®
179 C

PANTONE®
7513 C

PANTONE®
613

PANTONE®
110 M

David Bailey - Febbraio, 1967

periwinkle, sapphire or powder? Or red. Is it poppy, crimson, burgundy, brick, fuchsia, ruby, scarlet, coral, cherry, rose or cerise? A warm blue may have a hint of red in it; a dull red may have been dirtied with a little black.

Even those colours that we think of as non-colours, such as white and black, show a remarkable degree of variation. If you were to collect together in one place a number of white objects – for example, a piece of paper, a ceramic plate, a pillowcase, a porcelain cup, a piece of chalk, a jug of milk, a cup of flour – you might begin to see the extent to which white shades from ice-white or blue-white to palest grey or cream.

Paint manufacturers try to guide us in our choice by coming up with associative names for different shades, often as not making some reference to the natural world. One British company, which has researched historical paint colours and produces a heritage range in association with the National Trust, has an almost poetic approach to paint naming. 'Calamine', for example, is the same pale chalky pink as the lotion, paler than 'Ointment Pink' or 'Smoked Trout', while 'Elephant's Breath' is a pale pinkish grey.

On my desk I keep the three Pantone colour books, reference bibles for any designer. Everyone perceives colour a little differently and Pantone was founded in the early 1960s to address the increasing problem of achieving accurate colour matching in printing. The system enables anyone working with colour to identify, match and communicate their choices so that designers and producers or printers all speak the same colour language. Swatches or chips in the Pantone books come in coated, uncoated and matte finishes, so that matching can be as precise as possible.

Another invaluable resource consists of my jars of snippets and swatches of coloured cloths, trims and yarns that I have collected over the

A kitchen in an East London flat with its original decor, Formica table and tiles was the location for a S/S 2006 shoot.

MULTI   BI-COLOUR

469 m

459 m

385 m

171 m

169 m

7470
+
302

10 m or
11 m

BI-
COLO
18

years. Flat colour, either painted or printed onto paper, gives you one dimension; strips of fabric and pieces of threads and yarns provide another.

The first thing we do when we are starting a new collection is to come up with a palette of colours for the season, normally between ten and twelve different shades, arranged in two to three colourways. Naturally, colours will tend to be lighter and brighter for summer, and darker and richer for winter, in tune with the way people commonly respond to the change in seasons and the change in light.

How we arrive at a colour palette is difficult to put into words – so much is instinctive. People often find themselves drawn to the family of colours time after time, or form quite strong attachments to a particular shade for a limited period, almost like falling in love. 'Olive and Orange', the name of our new diffusion range, references two of the colours I am drawn to over and over again. Yet it is important to bring something new into the picture each season, and this is where it can be so rewarding to look at artists' work and other sources of inspiration, so that you broaden out your tastes and frames of reference. Our autumn/winter 2009 collection features purple, a colour I always swore I would never use, perhaps because of my association it with in the 1980s and the overuse of it with black, which is a very hard combination. What has restored purple to me is using it with browns and ochres. The combination is wonderful.

At this early stage the colour palette will consist of scraps of reference material, which may be Pantone chips, yarn or snippets of fabric, taped onto card. From these initial ideas we will proceed to assemble mood boards of imagery, collages of photographs, posters, paintings and other visual material to trigger design thoughts and suggest particular directions to develop in print.

Colour chart showing yarn colours and fabric swatches (left); Jars of colour swatches in my studio (previous pages).

mixing & matching

· · · · · · · · ·

Colour combination is an essential ingredient of pattern. The moment you put two colours together, even if they are tones of the same shade, or a graphic partnering of a solid colour with black or white, you begin to suggest relationships and design directions. Exploring colour combinations is endlessly fascinating.

When you are working with colour or building up your ideas into a mood board, you need conditions where there is a good quality of natural light. Making fine judgements and distinguishing between one shade and the next ideally requires daylight, north light if possible. Failing daylight, halogen light sources give the truest colour rendering and are closest to white light. Tungsten has a yellow cast and uncorrected fluorescent gives a greenish light that can distort colour relationships.

Tone plays as important a role as the precise blend of hues and is a function of how light or dark a colour is. Is it a pale yellow, or a rich, saturated yellow? Is it a green that contains so much white that barely a whisper of the colour remains, or is it a green that is so dark that it is almost as black as a pine forest at twilight?

Colour cards produced by paint manufacturers tend to be arranged tonally, in strips from the palest to the most intense versions of a particular shade. Taken as a starting point, this breadth of choice can be overwhelming. But the real value of colour cards, as with the Pantone books, is to enable you to match a colour reference as closely as possible. That's why it is important

Reflected Trees, Giant Stem and Boulevard prints in different colourways.

to start with the inspiration – the fabric swatch or the cutting torn out of a magazine – and then source the colour as accurately as you can.

Tonal difference plays an important role in our perception of colour and the way certain combinations work. To take an obvious example: a texture or finish will naturally affect the way we see a certain shade because of the way that light is reflected. Glossy or highly polished surfaces give colour an added intensity and sharpness. On the other hand, matte or soft finishes, which are not so reflective, have a more muted effect. For that reason, it isn't always possible to match colours precisely when you are putting together a decorative scheme, for instance.

Colour combinations based on tones of the same colour can be very effective in small doses, less so in larger applications, where they run the risk of being a little too enveloping and relentless. Graduated tones, from a distance, average out to a single colour, according to the proportion of light and dark in the mix, but close up have more character and depth than a solid shade.

Putting colours together that are near neighbours is another simple way of creating a successful combination. You might opt for a cool palette of blues, blue-greens and greys, or a warmer one of reds and pinks. The basic compatibility of a harmonious scheme or palette gives it a distinctive mood that can be very evocative and powerful. A combination of closely related warm colours has in-built pleasure and energy, while a cooler palette is calm and soothing.

Contrast is the essence of colour combination and begins to introduce a musical or structured quality that is immediately suggestive of pattern. A single solid shade and white or black can form the basis for very simple striped or spotted designs, or for a linear pattern where a shape is picked out from its background. Instead of white or black, cream or brown will give a gentler effect.

Previous pages: A selection of printed and laminated classic shoulder bags from the Etc diffusion ranges.

Another standard way of exploring colour contrast is to play around with complementary pairs. In their pure form, the complementary pairs of blue and red, orange and green, and yellow and purple are inherently vibrant – they jar against one another, vying for attention. One tried and tested method of coming up with a workable colour combination is to use lighter or darker tones of complementary colours with each other, along with shades that are achieved by blending the two colours together. It is important to retain a sense of crispness and definition, however, otherwise the result can look a little too staid, perhaps even a bit lifeless. The most exciting colour palettes always have an element of edginess and surprise.

When we are developing a palette for a particular season, we are looking to create a basic compatibility across the board, where each colour contributes something to the mix. At the same time, it is also a question of tweaking the palette so that the colours not only work together well but also come to life. Quite small adjustments can make a surprising difference. An element of playfulness is very important to me. If there are a number of dark, deep rich colours in the palette, we will always add an injection, a jolt, of a brighter and more irreverent shade to convey a sense of youthfulness and optimism, perhaps in the form of a fluorescent. What we are looking for is a feeling of fun and happiness, rather than a more sober formality and sophistication. This added jolt can also help to prevent a collection from being excessively coordinated.

Accent and proportion are also key factors to consider when you are working out how to put colours together. A good use of the vibrancy inherent in complementary pairs is in the form of accents or trim. A buttonhole edged with a contrasting colour, a contrasting rim on a bowl and similar types of detailing can give an added lift to a colour combination, or give a solid

Multi-stripe cardigan and Perforated Flower print bikini from S/S 2004 collection shot on location in my garden.

shade a greater degree of liveliness. One way of judging the effect of such accents is to play around with strips of colour and colour blocking. When we first introduced knitwear into our collection, many of the designs were based around the playfulness of colour accents. Little twists, such as having each cuff of a jumper in a different colour, provided an element of fun and surprise. A similar idea was the basis for another early knitwear collection where each colourway in the range had a different-coloured stripe arranged in a different combination. Simple, but a great way of expressing the pure pleasure of colour.

Shelves of vintage crockery from the S/S 2008 lookbook photoshoot.

print

print

· · · · · · · · ·

Pattern is powerful and transformative, adding rhythm and movement to the sensory experience of colour and texture. It can be rather stately and measured, suggestive of order and repose; flowing and branching, leading the eye onward; or lively and dancing, almost in a musical sense. Whichever is the case, there is something both joyful and infectious about it. And it is infinitely variable. Recolouring a pattern will naturally affect its impact. But differences in scale and proportion also have roles to play.

In the purest sense, pattern, like colour, is a way of delighting the eye. It sets up relationships between foreground and background, which gives us depths to peer into. It travels across a surface in a rhythmic way, which gives us paths to trace. It invites us to make connections, to take pleasure in order and arrangement, and to enjoy the drama of scale. Somehow it manages to bridge the gap between how things appear and the way they feel: a patterned fabric is always more than the sum of its constituent colours and the material or texture on which it is printed. At its best, pattern exists for its own sake. It may well be ornamental, but it is not simply a means of dressing things up.

Like colour, pattern took a back seat in the 1990s, both in interior design and in clothing. This was a time when we were all exhorted to 'chuck out the chintz' and many of us promptly did. While the direction of design during that period represented a welcome return to clean lines and modernity, after the various period revivals of the 1980s, in some respects there was also a tendency to go too far and throw the baby out with the bathwater.

Previous pages: The Pear print, with its clean, graphic quality, shows the impact of large-scale designs.

Early modernists at the beginning of the twentieth century, who similarly lived in largely pattern-free surroundings, saw ornament as a crime and something of this attitude may well have been the reason why pattern was dismissed when contemporary design came back into fashion. It is also true to say that there is always the risk of pattern being used indiscriminately and inappropriately – to unnecessarily prettify – and becoming almost devalued as a consequence. There are many ways in which you might put a pattern on, say, a toaster and create something eye-catching and appealing, but a wispy motif of wheat sheaves wouldn't be one of them.

To see pattern as simply an ornament, however, is to misunderstand it in a fundamental sense. Pattern exists in the world: it is part of the underlying mathematical structure or design of life. Just as our eyes are capable of making many fine colour judgements, we are predisposed to create order, to find pattern in what we see. We are always on the lookout for connections, just as one thought leads to another. To cut yourself off from pattern is like depriving yourself of a sense, or living without music.

A love of pattern has been a constant in my life – the way certain colours sing together, the rhythm of a repeat, the dynamism of scale. My own preference is for patterns that are strong, graphic and stylized, not overly sweet or too pretty-pretty, even where they are looser and painterly. But I am also aware that print needs space, in a collection, in our lives and in our surroundings. It's a question of getting the balance right.

Our shared visual vocabulary means that pattern is often expressive of a particular time, mood or place. It naturally evokes associations. Simple blue and white stripes, for example, have a jaunty, nautical appeal, while highly figurative, busy floral prints can summon up images of old-fashioned drawing rooms swathed in faded chintz. Red and white checked gingham immediately transports you to a Parisian café. Often associations are built on previous associations. Those tiny sprigged Laura Ashley floral patterns, for example, so evocative of the 1970s, are themselves reminiscent in scale and motif of early nineteenth-century fabric and wallpaper designs – which was no accident, as they echoed the retro fashion for Victorian style at the time.

Many patterns are so specific you could date-stamp them or pinpoint their origin to a particular locality or type of product. In part, this has much to do with particular palettes of colour, which evoke their own responses, but the other key elements of motif, scale and repeat also have a bearing. To take a perhaps rather poignant example, in nineteenth-century Ireland seamen and fishermen on the west coast typically wore Aran sweaters, which took their name from the Aran Islands in the Atlantic Ocean, where they were first produced. These were knitted out of unwashed wool that retained its natural oils and so were waterproof. There were a number of traditional stitch patterns, mostly of the cable type, but since the sweaters were usually knitted by fishermen's wives the patterns showed local or individual variations, or incorporated hand-stitched initials, which made it easier to identify those who had drowned at sea – a not infrequent occurrence, since the seas could be rough and few fishermen could swim. Like Aran knitting, tartan weaving is another type of generic pattern that has strong regional roots.

Harmonious pattern combinations, featured in 'You' magazine from 'The Mail on Sunday'.

Even patterns that have a strong historical or cultural flavour, and which would appear destined to remain no more than objects of curiosity for students of design, can be given a new lease of life by the simple means of recolouring them or changing their scale. In recent years, as wallpaper has come back into fashion, a number of companies have delved into their archives and done just that. A paisley design, for example, which might look indelibly Victorian in its original sombre colourway, can look fresh and modern when the motif is enlarged and the colours changed to a vibrant combination of green and blue, or pink and red. A far more radical form of reworking can be seen in Timorous Beasties' subversive take on the classic eighteenth-century fabric pattern, toile de Jouy, which transforms the typical miniature bucolic or pastoral scenes into sharply observed comments on the modern urban cityscape. While a particular pattern always enshrines a 'now', the whole nature of the way it is put together makes it infinitely adaptable at a subsequent date.

Although fabric and paper have been the traditional vehicles for pattern, there are other cultural and historical sources that can provide inspiration. Ceramic designs, for example, or particular styles of packaging can suggest ideas for motif and repeat. Over the years, after many happy hours foraging in junk shops and in markets, I have amassed quite a collection of vintage fabric remnants in all sorts of materials and designs. But I am just as likely to be inspired by a scrap of old-fashioned wallpaper used as a drawer liner, or a book illustrated with the work of Scandinavian product and furniture designers, as I am by what one might call more literal sources.

Nature is another great source of pattern ideas. The distribution of petals on a flower head, the spiral shape of seashells, the crystalline form of snowflakes, among many other natural structures, have been demonstrated

Natural inspiration: Alpine Forest print raincoat from the A/W 2006 collection shot on location in the French Alps.

to conform to the golden ratio. The golden ratio, or golden section, is the basis of the Fibonacci sequence, whereby each successive number is the sum of the previous two: 1:1:2:3:5:8. Fibonacci numbers are extremely common in nature, from petal numbers to the pattern of tree growth. Daisies, for example, quite often have 13, 21, 34, 55 or 89 petals, all of which are Fibonacci numbers. Pattern is there in the maths.

Go for a walk in the park or the countryside and you will see pattern everywhere – the radiating lines of a spider's web, picked out in beads of dew, the delicate tracery of veins in a leaf, the layering of sedimentary rock formations where they are exposed by the shore, the feathery wisps of clouds in the sky. In the wild, natural patterns are often a means of camouflage, from the dappled coat of a fawn that enables it to hide from its predators in a shady woodland, to the striped coat of a tiger that allows it to stalk its prey through the jungle. At the same time, the patterns you see on the coats, scales or feathers of many creatures can also be a means of exuberant display, with the eye-catching combinations of spots and stripes and banding designed to lure potential mates.

My take on nature has always been more abstract and graphic, filtered through my own modern aesthetic, which owes a great deal to mid-century design. This was a time when the traditional floral, typified by full-blown patterns smothered in cabbage roses, was transformed into something more fundamental, almost structural, with bare branches or seed heads arranged in tight grids taking the place of looser, blowsier and more representational designs. At the same time, nature as a source of inspiration was taken in its broadest sense, down to the microscopic levels of crystal structures or the double helix of DNA. The clean-lined modernity of such designs is very appealing to me, and so is their inherent sense of optimism and cheerfulness.

Just as the work of artists can provide inspiration for colour ideas, such sources can also suggest directions for print design. Painted (or sculpted) pattern is an obvious reference point – Edouard Vuillard's depictions of intensely patterned interiors and his renderings of wallpaper and dress fabric are one example. Less literally, it may be the manner in which the paint is laid down – the physical marks of the brushstrokes or chisel – that is evocative. The tiny multicoloured dots that make up the paintings of the pointillist Georges Seurat almost blur into abstraction on close inspection. Very different are the drips and splatters of a Jackson Pollock painting, or the diffused way in which dark, moody bands of colour shade into each other in paintings by Mark Rothko.

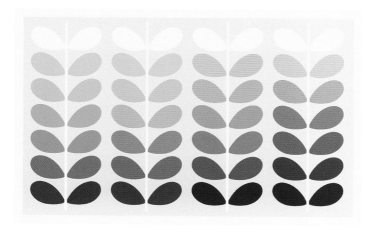

Natural Stem print notecard. Stem is a very versatile print and lends itself to a variety of different applications.

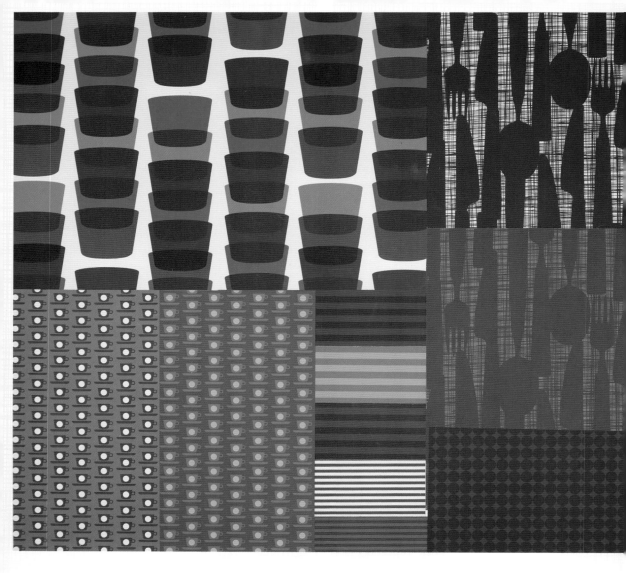

pattern families

· · · · · · · · ·

Just as there are literally thousands of colours, if our eyes could be taught to distinguish them, pattern comes in countless permutations, particularly when you take into account the basic variables of motif, colourway, repeat and scale. Yet common themes that particular families of pattern share can be identified, and these have been in existence ever since people began to represent the world around them, looking for connections and ordering what they saw into sequences.

All pattern is in some sense geometric, given that its very nature involves the repetition of a motif or design at regular given intervals. Stripes, spots or checks, where repeat and motif are more or less indivisible, are the archetypical geometric patterns. Various combinations of curves and lines and solid shapes also gives us zigzags, spirals, concentric circles, lozenges, octagons and many other types of motif that share the same mathematical foundation. The absolute beauty of pure geometric forms was explored by various designers associated with the Bauhaus, notably the weavers Anni Albers and Gunta Stöltzl, before pattern-making of any description was discouraged.

Many geometric patterns are based on regularly shaped elements or motifs arranged in some form of a grid – think of tiling, such as the classic example of a black and white marble floor, or mosaic, or the pieced squares or hexagons of a patchwork quilt. In terms of geometrically patterned fabrics, such designs often owe their origin to the way textiles are or have been produced – the alternating rows of knitting, for example, or the crisscross of warp and weft threads in woven ones.

A print board featuring prints and stripes in different colourways for A/W 2007.

Layered montage of outfits on the front cover of the *A/W 2007* lookbook.

Geometric prints can be deceptively simple. A spot or grid print, for example, can vary enormously not only according to colour but also its distribution across a background, as well as its scale. Equal, regular spacing will have a different impact to random or staggered arrangements.

Patterns that paint a picture, or that describe recognizable scenes, have been a common preoccupation of designers at various times and in various cultures. William Morris, perhaps the most famous pattern designer of all time, was determined to capture a sense of nature's vitality in his designs, many of which were based on close observations of native English flowers, leaves and stems, arranged across a ground in S-shapes or diagonally so as to be suggestive of growth. Morris's designs represented an important break from what had previously been seen as naturalistic – those mid-Victorian designs that attempted to convey realism through elaborate detailing and shading, and which could be so claustrophobic. A Morris print always retained an awareness of surface, which was not to say that it was flat in effect.

Representational designs may be more or less realistic. In general, however, you don't have to work too hard to spot the point of reference or identify the source of the motif. The arrival of digital printing, which has allowed photographic images to be transferred onto a whole range of surfaces or products, from mugs to tiles, has brought a whole new dimension into play.

For me, stylization is the heart of pattern design and is strongly associated with contemporary prints, sometimes to the point of abstraction. Distilling a form, natural or man-made, into its basic elements, while maintaining a degree of recognition, gives certain poise and tension to a design, so that it reads in two distinct ways at the same time. This tension can be enhanced by layering motifs or by interlocking them to such an extent that there is an element of concealment.

Playing with scale: Variations of the Car print from the A/W 2003 print board.

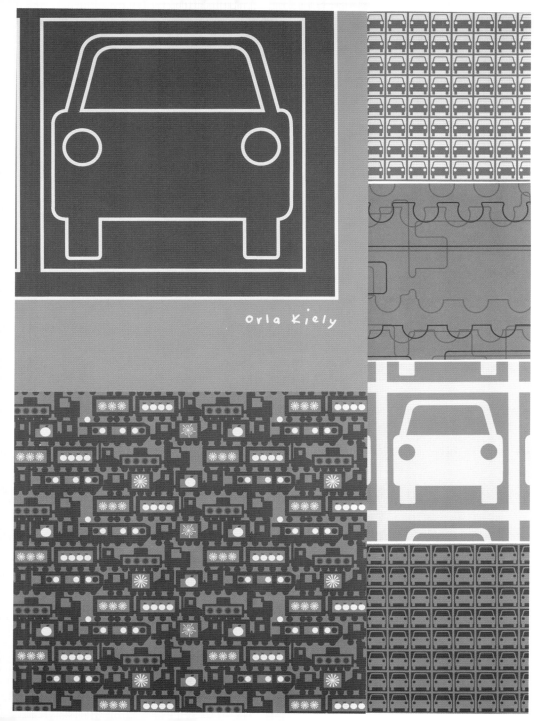

Orla Kiely

building blocks

• • • • • • • • •

If a colour palette is the building block of pattern, the motif – or motifs – is a fundamental element of print. Although, in most cases, a motif will never be conceived in isolation from the scale at which it will be used or the way it will be repeated across a surface, some form of image, theme or drawing is a natural starting point for design.

Print is the essence of what we do and what our label is known for. Yet colour is the root of it all and it is only after the colour palette has been decided upon that we will begin to think about patterns for the coming season. Again, as with colour, it all starts with inspiration, trawling the memory banks for shapes and forms that might spark a new direction. It is important to have a theme or an element or two to anchor a print collection. For spring/summer 2010, for example, it was sailboats, along with sand dune flora, in part inspired by the artist Patrick Heron's work in Cornwall.

Brainstorming, undertaking research and assembling images is followed by sketching and drawing, with the team communicating back and forth until the ideas begin to take shape. Very early on sketches will be put onto the computer, where the design grid provides a spatial framework to locate the motifs and hold them in place.

Then it is a question of simplifying and refining the basic motifs and working them up into patterns. Sometimes a happy accident can affect the way a motif or pattern is developed. While we were working on that sailboat print for the spring/summer 2010 season, for example, the screen froze on

Print board from the Etc diffusion range: Tonal Stem, Linear Flower Oval and Stacked Cups in different colourways.

the computer and we could only view the image in an outline or scribble form, which I liked as much as the other finished artworks we had been developing. It had a spontaneity that was instantly appealing.

Between the purely abstract or geometric print and the more conventionally representational design lies an interesting area to explore. Although many of our prints make some form of reference to nature – flowers, trees, leaves, fruit – others feature motifs drawn from more surprising sources, such as linear drawings of everyday objects – cutlery (flatware), cups and saucers, or tonal prints of stacked glassware. Our tiny teacup print, for example, was inspired by a photograph of 1960s crockery, where the cup handles had a characteristically squared-off profile.

For me, a touch of humour and quirkiness is important in design. In many cases, it's the humour of recognition, of seeing the familiar in a different way. Sometimes, it's the element of discovery, where you suddenly see the origins of a design concealed within a repeat. More often, it's the irrepressible feeling of fun and light-heartedness that raises a smile. What I love about pattern is its ability to convey happiness, which is a much underrated aspect of design.

Over the years, we have been fortunate to work with the Tate to produce designs to accompany various exhibitions, including one on Josef Albers, and one on the Bauhaus, developing products across the board, from umbrellas to bags and wallets. For our first collaboration with the Tate, when we were asked to do a range to accompany an exhibition of 1960s art, we came up with a print based on a stylized Martian, a reference to 1960s sci-fi. The print is quite dense and small in scale, so the alien theme is not overt: it is only when you look closer that you realize what it is. Garden Tortoise, another design with a hidden element, showed a pair of tortoises kissing.

From the buyers' point of view, one of our more eccentric prints was Car, which came out in autumn/winter 2003. The print was a small-scale repeat of a stylized drawing or pictogram of a car, seen front on, so small in scale that the pattern almost read as a texture. As with the Martian and Garden Tortoise prints, it was only obvious that the motif was a car when you looked at it closely. The initial reactions of the buyers were not as promising as we had hoped and orders were down. But once the bags featuring the Car print were delivered to the stores, they flew off the shelves and the phone started ringing with reorders. What this illustrates is that as a designer you need the confidence to trust your own taste and hope that others share it.

Part of the process of building up each design involves seeing whether anything is missing, whether you have gone too far or not far enough. Sometimes a print will need a dot, a line or a texture to sharpen it and bring it into focus; sometimes it will need to be pared back or opened up a little. It is often a good sign if an idea comes quickly and is resolved quickly, as it did with Stem. But, quick or slow, there comes a time I call 'cracking it', when you know the print is good. This is the time during the development process when you know you have done enough and it's time to stop. The pattern is there. It's a very nice feeling.

Playing with scale brings drama to print design. Many of our designs are quite large in scale, which gives them added 'oomph' or graphic impact. But the product or end use always needs to be considered. A print that can seem big in scale on a dress, for example, may seem small on a wallpaper or furnishing fabric, which is why you should always photocopy the design and build up the repeat to gauge the effect of a pattern in context. Changing the scale of a design from a previous season can be a good way of breathing new life into it.

Large-scale designs bring a different dynamic to pattern placement. When you use a print with a large motif in a small application, for example, to make a purse or wallet, the necessary cropping of the print introduces an element of asymmetry and abstraction, which can be interesting and appealing. Our womenswear collections tend to feature simple silhouettes, and using a large-scale print is a good way of giving an easy dress shape an added degree of vitality and youthfulness.

Some of our designs incorporate large- and small-scale elements in the same print, which can be a good way of drawing the eye in and investing a design with a particular richness and sense of rhythm. One small simple flower shape that was used as a motif in one of our collections also appeared layered and built up into a larger floral pattern in a companion print. On the very smallest of scales, print becomes a texture or a colour, with the graphic nature of the design only really discernible when you get close. A black and white pin-dot pattern, for example, will read as a textural grey from a distance.

A motif or a drawing may be the building block of print, but it is not the full story. Pattern can be complex, intricate and rich in detail, or open, free-flowing, even a little jazzy, but what holds every print together is the repeat.

All too often, when people are thinking about creating a pattern, they focus their attention on a theme or some other isolated design element, forgetting that the essence of print is repetition. To design patterns, you have to think in pattern, you have to see the continuation right from the outset. This is a particular skill that comes with practice and experience and it is all to do with training the eye to make visual judgements. When I do a rough sketch of a print, for example, I will always repeat the motif across the paper and then cut it off from the rest of the page by drawing an enclosing frame

Previous pages: The repeat, whether scattered, layered or gridded, is the essence of pattern. Print boards for S/S 2006.

Our Flower Blossom print translated into bedlinen.

Flower Blossom print skirt in a Teal colourway.

around it, rather like a window, so I can get a sense of what the full coverage will look like. The relationship between foreground and background is what gives a print its dynamism, its rhythm and its sense of movement.

A repeat has to do with the way a motif covers the ground, how it is arranged across a surface. Repeats can be open, with the motif distributed across the surface so that plenty of background shows through – a 'ditzy' version of this is where the motif itself is cute and small in scale – or they can be closed or tessellated so that there is less space or background. Some repeats are very obviously gridded, staggered in a half drop, aligned or otherwise held in a tight framework; others are looser and appear more random. Another element that involves repetition is layering, where a print is built up with elements placed on top of one another. Layering is a good way of giving a quality of depth to an otherwise simple design.

Whichever form a repeat takes, you may need to make adjustments to get the right effect of evenness and to prevent another pattern from creeping in where none was intended. The eye is naturally drawn to empty space, and sometimes unwanted stripes or holes can appear in the areas of a print where the pattern is denser. Years ago, when I was working for a company in New York that designed ranges of wallpaper, one of my jobs was to paint up a single repeat of the pattern on a page. But it is difficult to assess how a pattern will work in terms of a repeat from a piece of paper that is 6cm (2⅜ inches) square. My best friend was the photocopier – I would photocopy the *croquis* and stick them together, nine at a time, so that I ended with one in the middle. Then I would pin up the sheet and view it from a distance, which gave me the chance to see if any holes or stripes had appeared in the repeat. If there were, I would have to add elements or move them around so that the holes or stripes were filled.

Overleaf: A poster showing a selection of products from the S/S 2004 collection.

a b c d

1

2

3

4

5

6

7

8

9

orla kiely

spring / summer collection 2004

print combinations

• • • • • • • • •

At different periods of time people's tolerance for the density of pattern has varied widely. The Victorians famously lived in a riot of pattern, with different designs competing for attention in the same room. Lace at the window might have been overlaid with brocade drapery, paisley shawls with needlepoint chair backs, dense naturalistic wallpaper above the dado (chair) rail with an embossed design of a quite different nature below. At the opposite end of the spectrum, pattern has often appeared in more modern surroundings as a lone focal point, perhaps in the form of a rug. A similar reticence can be seen in the way people have tended to wear pattern in recent years, with prints rarely being seen in combination.

Combining prints brings a whole new dimension into play. It may take more confidence and a greater degree of experimentation to put prints together, but it can be very rewarding and much richer in effect without becoming at all stifling or overwhelming.

Print combination is the essence of our collections. When we are working up designs for a new season, we always ask ourselves in a very practical way how many prints we are going to need, whether they will be big or small, multicoloured or linear. So often I see portfolios of students' work where there are pages and pages of very similar prints, done on a very similar scale. While you do want designs to work together in a collection, an element of contrast is crucial so that you create a balance across the board. Each print should also be sufficiently different from the others so that it can stand on its own.

Mixing and matching: Striped Petal print dress and Wallflower print hat, S/S 2008.

The way to achieve this is by exploiting all the variables and working with opposites – in other words, partnering busy patterns with emptier ones, linear prints with textural designs, large-scale prints with smaller repeats. You might have one very colourful print alongside others that are more subdued, or prints that have a dense coverage partnered with those that are thinner and lighter. You want them all to sit happily together and to tell the same story, but you don't want too obvious a coordination or too much similarity.

Texture is another key element. In this context, it is not so much the texture of the fabric on which the design will be printed, although that is also crucial, but the way texture can be suggested through broken or hatched lines or what one might call doodles or scribbles. Such textural effects can be cut out and contained as a graphic shape, just as you would use solid colour; alternatively, you can reverse or punch a clean shape out of a textural background.

Also useful when you are building up a collection, and looking for that elusive combination of balance and variety, are simple geometric patterns – stripes, checks, spots, squares and lines. While these patterns are so elemental as to be almost free of a design signature, there are nevertheless many ways in which you can put your individual stamp on things, using colour, shifts of scale and different types of application. A row of spots punched out of leather, for example, has a very different impact to a row of spots printed onto fabric. Broad multicoloured stripes have all the cheeky appeal of the English seaside; narrow red or navy stripes on a white background epitomize a certain type of French chic.

Print combination is at the heart of our collections. Outfits from S/S 2009.

Above and beyond the way a collection for a single season works, is the way prints work together and contribute to the label or brand as a whole. We keep all our print boards from season to season so that we can keep our eye on achieving precisely this sense of consistency, even while we are exploring new directions.

When you are designing a pattern, it is important to understand the technical process of printing in order to anticipate problems. This type of training forms the basis of many art school courses in fashion and textiles and provides essential hands-on experience.

In fine art printing, the type of process you choose will give you a different quality of tone or line – with soft ground etching, for example, you can reproduce the soft texture of a pencil line, whereas hard ground etching results in a line of needle-fine clarity. Similarly, the challenge of designing for textile printing is to achieve the result you want within the parameters of a given process.

With a few exceptions, most of our designs are screen-printed and the screens are developed in the factory – we don't use a digital process, which suits photographic prints better than it suits the type of graphic work we do. Each colour entails a separate screen, so the more colours in the print, the more expensive and demanding it will be to produce. Once the screens are made, the fabric is printed using a rotary process. Printing dyes are fed into a tube that rolls along the surface of the fabric. These tubes only come in certain sizes and diameters, so this affects the size of the repeat you can produce – a repeat cannot be bigger or smaller than a certain size due to the mathematics of fitting it into the available surface area –

Previous pages: A 1970s beach house on the Sussex coast was the location for the S/S 2008 campaign.

which can sometimes be frustrating, but must be considered at the outset.

Other limitations can come from the type of design you produce. While I do like loose and painterly patterns, it is fair to say that my work has never been messy. Clean lines and graphic shapes, however, can be trickier to produce and are less tolerant of error. As each new screen is overlaid on the previous printing, there is always the risk of mis-registration if one colour is too close to another, with the result that you might lose the shape a little. Either you have to leave a small gap to allow for that possibility, or build in a small overprint to ensure that the colours overlap. One pattern that we produced for spring/summer 2008 was a stripy petal design where concentric lines had to meet more or less exactly to create the flower shape. That was a demanding print to produce.

At the right scale and in the right colours, pattern lends itself to a host of applications. Pattern tends to be synonymous in most people's minds with textiles and it is certainly the case that fabric has always been an important application for print. Paper is another.

The concept of unity in interior design, which first arose in eighteenth-century France, saw pattern in fabric and wallpaper begin to converge, so that, for example, you might see a motif repeated across the flat surface of a wall that was originally derived from a characteristic feature of a particular type of fabric. But all patterns are not equally transferable from one type of application to another. The patterns you put on a bag, for instance, need to have a certain degree of strength and clarity – they need an element of structure and punchiness. Our sales team tried to persuade us that a small print of drifting boats that we produced for spring/summer 2010 should appear on

a bag, but to me, while the pattern worked beautifully on a silk dress, it didn't have enough impact for a bag. The same is true of prints for wallpaper. Pretty, small-scale floral designs lose impact on such a scale and become a little too sugary, although they might work really well on a dress or a top.

One of the challenges for print designers is to get their name and work recognized. The world is full of wonderful patterns and it is not always clear who has designed what – a design student might be able to pick out a pattern designed by Lucienne Day or Barbara Brown from other contemporary textiles produced in the 1950s and 1960s, but for many people, their prints might simply register as examples of retro designs. One of the advantages of conceiving print for specific applications – which for us, in the beginning, was bags – is that you stand a greater chance of developing your business on the strength of it.

Varying the scale of a pattern is a good way to combine prints. Dresses, cardigan and coat from the S/S 2004 collection.

print gallery

· · · · · · · · ·

The following pages feature a gallery of Orla Kiely prints, spanning the past ten years and specially selected from our archive. In the majority of cases, we have photographed the actual fabric – whether it is textured cotton canvas, silk, twill or crepe – on which the print originally appeared to give an accurate sense of scale, proportion, colour and texture. Some digital print files are also included in the selection.

These prints have been used in various applications – on clothing, bags and homeware, for example. We have also included a number of designs that we produced for special projects in collaboration with Tate Galleries.

A special project for Tate Galleries, 2004, this martian soft toy is made in Martian print on grey cotton canvas.

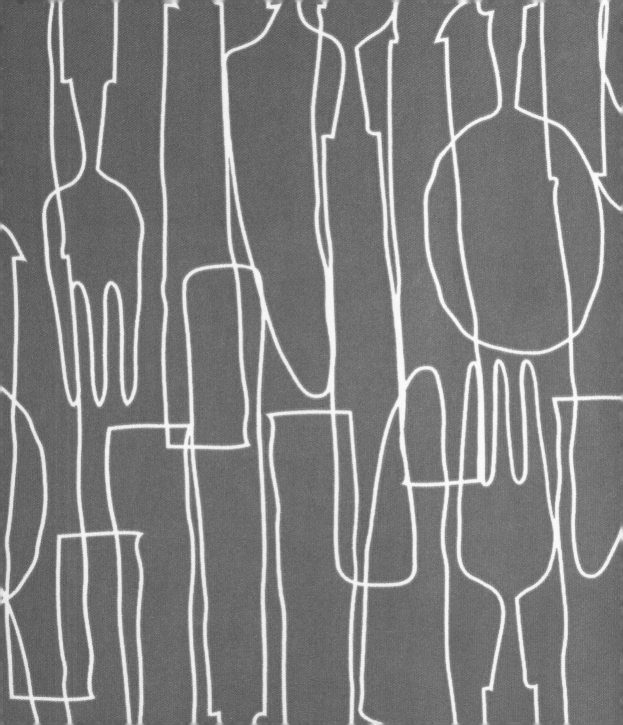

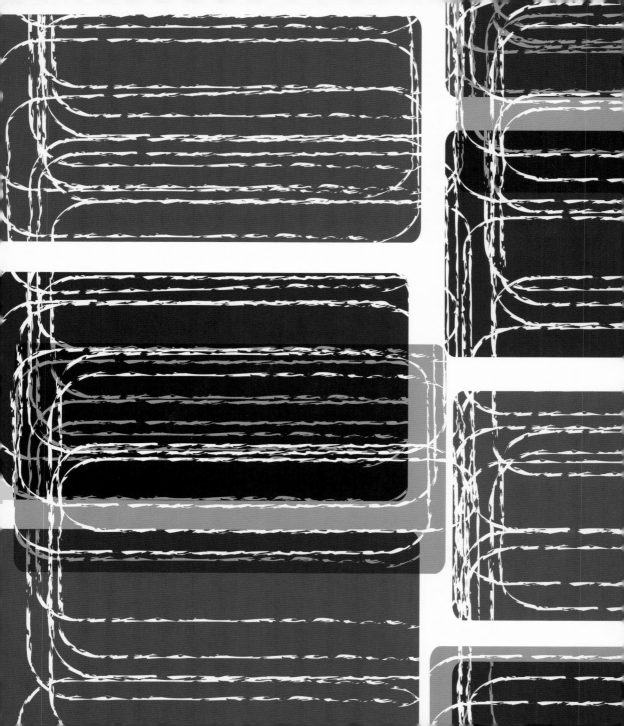

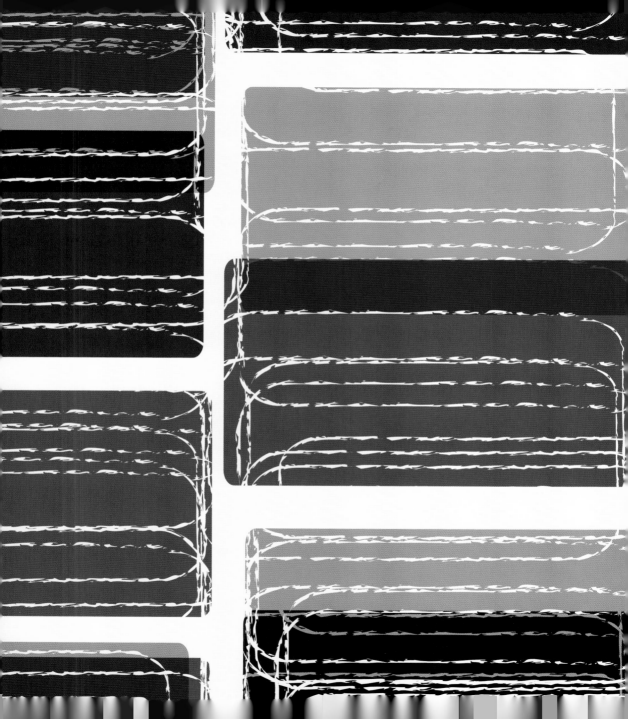

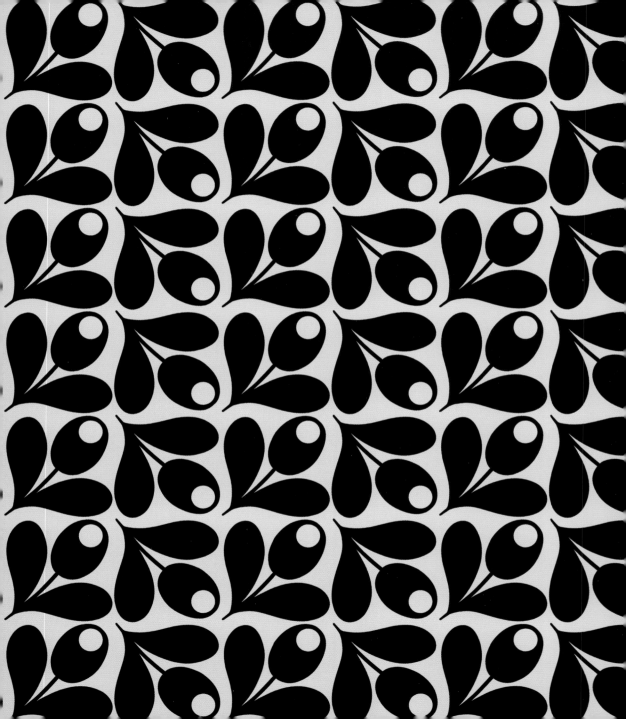

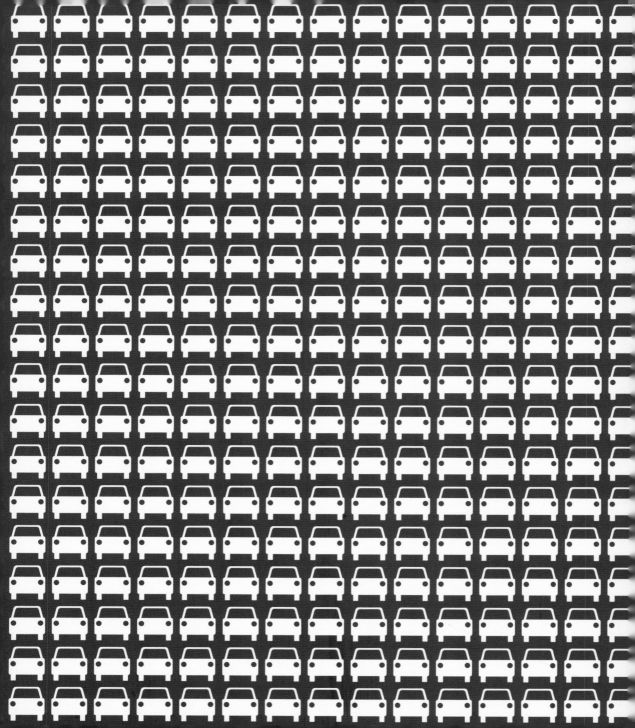

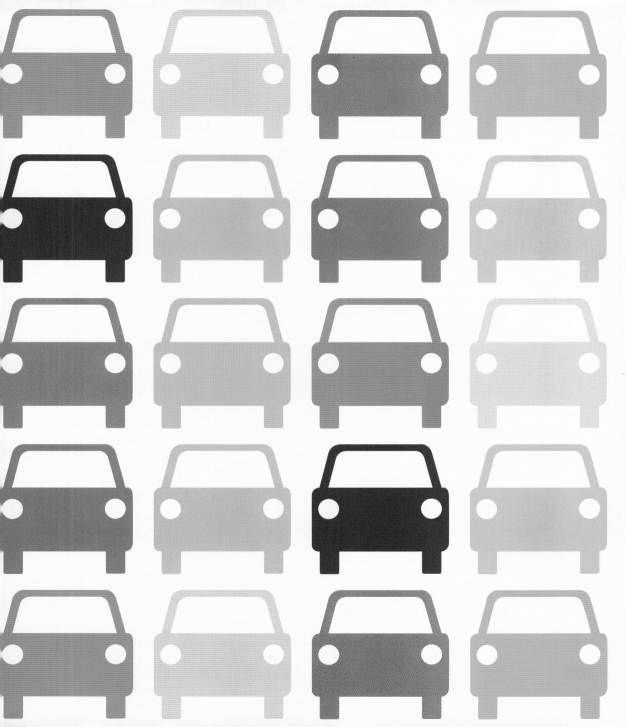

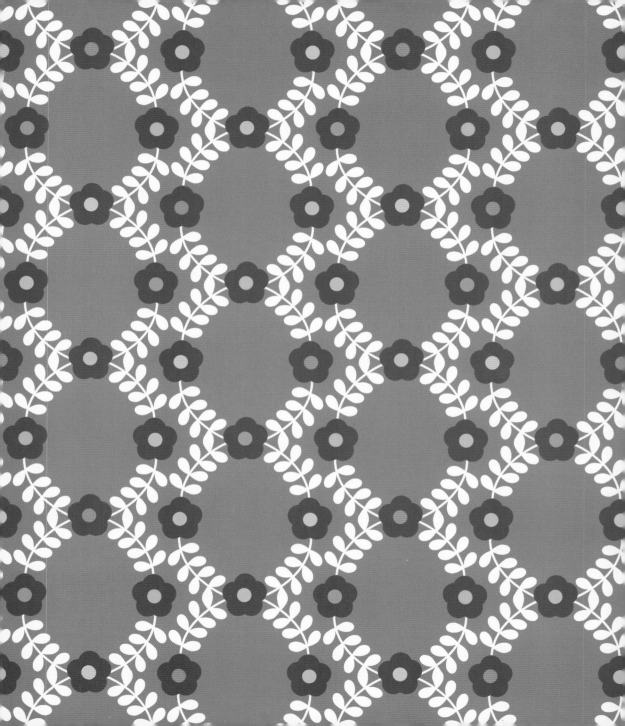

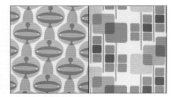
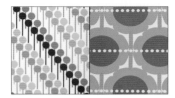
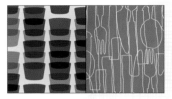

Page 164: Martian print in Green. Special project
for Tate Galleries, 2004.
Page 165: Layered Square Flower print
in Orange and Grey S/S 2005.

Page 166: Boulevard Print in Multi, S/S 2004.
Page 167: Perforated Flower print in Orange
S/S 2006.

Page 168: Glass Tumblers print in Burnt Orange,
A/W 2007.
Page 169: Linear Cutlery print in Olive, A/W 2007.

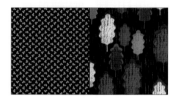
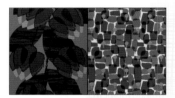

Page 170: Tiny Tumblers print in Cocoa,
A/W 2007.
Page 171: Glass Tumblers print in Kingfisher
A/W 2007.

Page 172: Ditsy Clover print in Graphite,
A/W 2009.
Page 173: Crayon Forest print in Dark Oak,
A/W 2009.

Page 174: Winter Clematis print in Moss and
Fuchsia, A/W 2009.
Page 175: Aerial View print in Glade, A/W 2009.

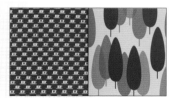
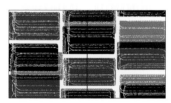

Page 176: Tiny Teacup print in Slate, A/W 2004.
Page 177: Alpine Forest print in Ruby,
A/W 2006.

Page 178-9 : Colourblock print in Walnut.
Special project for Tate Galleries, 2008.

Page 180: Acorn Cup print in Black, A/W 2010.
Page 181: Acorn Cup placement print in Multi
(for use on silk scarf), A/W 2010.

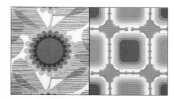

Page 182: *Giant Sunflower print in Raspberry, S/S 2009.*
Page 183: *Garden Tortoise print in Strawberries and Cream, S/S 2009.*

Page 184: *Giant Dahlia print in Navy, S/S 2007.*
Page 185: *Multi Rhododendron print in Ink, S/S 2009.*

Page 186: *Beach Flora print in Sea Green, S/S 2010.*
Page 187: *Boat Sketch print in Charcoal, S/S 2010.*

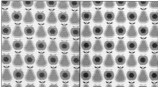

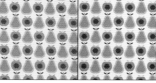

Page 188: *Multi Stem print, S/S 2008.*
Page 189: *Flower Abacus print in Slate, S/S 2008.*

Page 190: *Apples and Pears print in Green, S/S 2002.*
Page 191: *Apples and Pears print in Warm Grey, S/S 2002*

Page 192: *Flower Oval print in Grey for homeware collection, 2009.*
Page 193: *Balcony Spot print in Thistle, A/W 2008.*

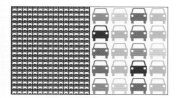

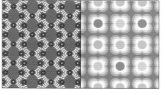

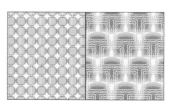

Page 194: *Small Car print in Brown, A/W 2003.*
Page 195: *Big Car Print in Multi S/S 2008.*

Page 196: *Multi Lattice Flower print in Birch. Special project for a Puffin Designer Classic book cover 2010.*
Page 197: *Primrose print in Mink for fragrance packaging, 2010.*

Page 198: *Small Spot print in Yellow. Special project for Tate Galleries, 2006.*
Page 199: *Bold Layered Square print in Ochre. Special project for Tate Galleries, 2006.*

collections

collections

· · · · · · · · ·

The rhythm of our working year is dictated by the fashion cycle, and the timing of the shows at which the autumn/winter and spring/summer collections are presented. In theory that ought to mean working for about half the year on each collection, yet because of the way the shows are scheduled, along with the demands of the production process and the interruption of the Christmas break, in practice we have about three months to produce an autumn/winter range and five months for spring/summer.

Because these schedules interlock, at any one moment we will be working on two seasons side by side. While we are putting the final touches to the print designs for a collection that will be available in a year's time, we will still be receiving production samples for the up-and-coming season, or creating promotional material to go along with it in the form of 'lookbooks' or short films to show on our website. We will also be producing designs for bed linen and homeware, working on special projects, and developing designs for our diffusion ranges of clothing and bags, as well as recolouring or rescaling prints from our archive.

All this means working to very tight deadlines and under a certain degree of pressure. Time management is key. It is certainly fairly relentless, and you can't jump out of the cycle, but the great reward of this business is that you are always doing something different and each day there is a new challenge.

The first four weeks we spend working on a new collection is a period of intense creativity and planning. During this short time, we will have

Previous pages: A selection of lookbook and campaign images taken over the years.

brainstormed the direction for the season, created the colour palette, selected the base cloths and leather, chosen yarns for knitwear and built a range plan for both bags and ready-to-wear. Alongside that, we will have determined how many prints we need and on which cloths. The result of all this effort will be two A0 boards on which all the artwork and their colourways are collated and displayed.

The next stage is putting the samples into work. The artwork and instructions go off to the factory, along with as much reference material as we can put together to help the printers understand what we are trying to create. As well as the artwork for the print designs, this reference material will include swatches – scraps of fabric and yarns – colour references and written instructions.

Three weeks later we see what are called the first 'strike-offs' – the first prints on the correct fabrics. The strike-off stage is always a moment of truth, a chance to see how your designs work when they are translated into printed textiles. At this stage, we might need to tweak a print to help overcome a problem of registration, for example. Sometimes a print will have turned out slightly differently from what we had expected and the change will be welcome. Most of our attention, however, will be focused on ensuring that the colour balance is absolutely right. A slight shift in the colour balance can make all the different between a print that is full of life and vitality and one that is flat and uninteresting.

Overleaf: A/W 2010; simply styled lookbook images to show the collection on the body.

While we are waiting for the first strike-offs and for a couple of weeks after we receive them, we will be coming up with designs for that season's knitwear, clothing, bags and other accessories. The team will pool their ideas and sources of influence, produce sketches and drawings, and we will discuss them together, eventually picking the ones we like. These designs then go off to the pattern cutter who makes the 'toiles' – the basic designs made up in plain fabric, often calico.

When the toiles are ready, we fit them on a model, who is a good size UK 10 (US 6), and assess them in detail. We may change the detailing of a collar shape on a coat, for example, or decide to line it with a print. Or we may decide to produce a certain dress shape in two different prints. Once we are satisfied with the pattern shapes, they are sent to the factory to be made up into samples.

Economies of scale mean that nowadays we can work with larger, more cost-effective producers because we are able to order in larger quantities, and a typical sample run will be 50m (54¾ yards) of each print. We are lucky to work with really good people from all over the world on both the supply and production side of the business.

The arrival of the first samples in the studio is another moment of truth. Our 'fit' model comes into the studio again to try on the collection and we can see exactly how a dress hangs on the body, whether we have got the proportions right or whether an element needs further adjustment. It is not always easy to envisage the impact of trim, accent or detailing early on in the design process and quite often at this stage we will change a few minor things – the colour of the buttons, say, or we will add a patterned trim for extra definition.

The corrected samples are what we show at Paris and London Fashion Weeks. A full collection for us is about 100 individual items, including all the

Striped silk cardigan with print panels and organza frill front blouse from S/S 2010 ad campaign.

colourways. The collection should be focused and tell a consistent story. Any more extensive and you start to dilute the message you are trying to get across.

After the shows, we have an eight-week selling window before we close our books. For any business, but particularly a fashion business, it is vital to meet your delivery dates and sufficient time must be left for production so that goods reach the shops at the right time. Occasionally things go wrong – a mill delivering fabric late to the printers really puts pressure on the schedule – but the bottom line is that orders must be fulfilled by the agreed date, come what may.

Fisherman print dress in Pebble colourway (left) and Drifting Boats print dresses (above) from S/S 2010.

material world

· · · · · · · · · ·

Translating designs from the flat page or screen into accessories or items of clothing destined to be worn on the body brings elements of texture, volume, line and proportion into play. It is possible to design bags or clothing before you have devised the prints for that season, or chosen the fabrics on which they will be displayed, but it is much more difficult. We always know when we are designing a dress, say, or a bag, what the print will be, if any, and which material or fabric the piece will be made of. Different prints and fabrics naturally suggest different ways in which they can be used.

What texture brings to pattern is an extra dimension of physicality, depth and character. It grounds print in the real material world of touch, weight and volume. Time is also part of the equation. How a particular material ages, how it responds to wear, how appropriate it is from a practical point of view for a particular use are all factors to consider. So, too, are questions of maintenance and aftercare.

Arguably pattern and texture overlap to a significant degree; they are certainly closely allied. This is related to the use of textural pattern in print design – hatchings, scribbles and doodles visually suggest a ridged or woven surface. On its own, texture, like solid colour, can be a way of introducing restraint and breathing space into a collection, in the same way as it mediates between highly coloured or intensely patterned surfaces in the interior. Sometimes texture can be the design story in itself – our shaggy Mongolian bag, from one of our early collections, was all about tactile appeal.

A selection of looks from the S/S 2010 lookbook. Each collection must be coherent, but include contrast and variety.

As with colour and print, contrast or variety is very important. Combining rough textures with smooth ones, shiny ones with matte, ridged with embossed, may be less overt than a colour palette based around vibrant complementary shades or a print collection that plays about with dramatic shifts in scale, but it is an equally important means of conveying richness and variety.

You can't appreciate textural variety properly or fully understand the particular qualities of specific materials by looking through the pages of a catalogue or gazing at images on a screen. You have to use your sense of touch, you have to feel the fabric, and gather it together to see how it drapes, folds or creases. This is where samples are so useful, in fashion as much as in interior design.

When you are working with textiles a significant part of the job is sourcing suppliers and going to shows to see the ranges on offer. Première Vision in Paris, for example, the world's leading fabric show, is where designers and producers exhibit their ranges twice a year, and where a print or fashion designer can connect with an Italian manufacturer of wool, or an Austrian supplier of lace, or an Irish company specializing in tweeds. Lineapelle, a leather trade show also held twice a year in Bologna, performs the same function for tanneries, as well as the suppliers of all the components, handles and other details that go into bags and shoes.

After the colour palette has been decided for a forthcoming season and while the prints are themselves at an early stage of development at the studio, we will be visiting these shows to see the suppliers we are going to be working with and to find new and interesting cloths. Assembling swatches of fabric or leather focuses design ideas very sharply. Later, during the production cycle, there is more liaising to be done by the production team, who will visit factories and mills to oversee progress and assemble information about how specific fabrics perform and how they need to be maintained and cared for – information that needs to be printed on garment or bag labels.

By the time we have come up with our final prints for a season we will have already made decisions about which prints will be printed onto which cloths. We will know, for example, that a particular big leafy print is destined to be produced in silk crepe, that a checked design will be on a tweed, that a crisp, graphic design is going to be printed onto cotton and laminated. In almost all instances, we will be fairly confident that if a print looks good as an artwork on a board, it is going to look even better when it is produced as a fabric.

Our ability to make these decisions, and make them rapidly, almost instinctively, comes down to experience and the knowledge of how different materials behave. It means understanding what a smooth, glossy and highly reflective finish will contribute to a particular design, or how a coarser or ribbed weave will affect depth of colour and pattern definition. There is inevitably an element of trial and error about the process to begin with. In our very first print collection, which included our geometric oval print, it proved very difficult to achieve the results we wanted when the design was printed onto wool. The particular wool we had chosen was dense and not very absorbent, and the factory was not able to get the dyes to penetrate the material as well as we might have hoped. With texture and material quality, as with much else in design, you learn as you go on.

While most people are not going to find themselves wandering around a trade fair, hunting down suppliers for a production run, the same principles of research apply. To make an informed selection of any material, whether it is a type of flooring, a wall covering or fabric to be used for soft furnishing, means doing the legwork, seeing what is out there and making judgements based on what lies deeper than surface and appearance.

My preference is to use natural fibres have an unmistakeable pedigree. Silk, lambswool, linen, cotton, cashmere and mohair each have their own distinct properties, but all are united by the fact that they feel good next to the skin. They don't all feel the same, or perform in the same way, but they do provide a high degree of tactile pleasure. Crucially, natural fibres are 'transpirational', which means that they breathe. For any application where a fabric will come in close contact with the skin — whether that is in the form of clothing, bed linen or bath linen — this quality is an important asset, as it allows the body to regulate its temperature and remain comfortable.

My preference is to use natural fibres in our collections wherever possible, although we may select some materials that include a small proportion of polyamide or nylon in the blend to structure the body of the fabric. Obviously, for certain applications — umbrellas, for example — synthetic materials are preferable for overriding practical reasons, but natural materials generally score much higher for all-round quality and character for the bulk of a collection. For me, it is also very important that a fabric will take print and colour well, and also that it will hold its shape.

Within the broad parameters of each particular type of fabric — cotton, say, or silk — there is immense variety according to specific types of weave or finish. The way a fabric is woven also contributes another dimension to print. Pattern will register sharply and flatly on smooth cotton weaves such as poplin; on a relief or textured cotton, such as hopsack, where the ribbing of

Ditsy Clover print raincoat from A/W 2009 featured in Lula magazine issue no.9.

the vertical and horizontal warp and weft is very apparent, the effect will be softer and have more depth. There is also great potential where different natural fibres are blended. A silk/linen blend, for example, may offer a special quality and perform differently in certain circumstances than either of its constituents would do on their own.

One of my favourite cloths is cotton, a practical and very fresh fabric for everyday. Cotton and pattern might have been made for each other. The crispness of the fabric's texture is echoed by the way it takes print so cleanly. For designs that are graphic by their nature, or that rely on precise colour separation in the screen-printing process, which many of ours are and do, cotton is the ideal surface to print on. It also dyes very well and is capable of representing shades and tones to a high degree of accuracy and definition.

Cotton approximates to a generic term for what is in reality a broad family of materials, from gauze-like muslin to puckered seersucker, from denser and heavier furnishing fabrics to soft terry towelling. All cotton fabrics are absorbent, which makes them cool next to the skin in hot weather. Such qualities can be further enhanced or altered by the nature of the weave. Seersucker, for example, is woven in such a way as to produce a puckered surface that stands away from the skin. Waffle weave, with its honeycombed surface, is highly absorbent, which makes it an excellent choice for bath linen, while brushed cotton is exceptionally soft and warm, owing to the way air is trapped between the raised fibres.

I also love silk, which has long been associated with luxury and richness, and highly prized for its sensuous texture. With a strength that belies its lightness and apparent delicacy, it also takes dye very well owing to its great absorbency. Printed onto silk, colours attain a particular lustre and jewel-like intensity.

Previous pages: Selection of looks from A/W 2009 lookbook (left) and Ditsy Clover print dress (right).

Depending on the weave, silk can be slippery and sleek or more overly textured, as is the case with 'raw' or 'slubbed' silk, where raised fibres and irregularities produce a rougher feel. From structural duchesse or taffeta with their paper-like quality, to silk crepe with all its drape, and from silk jersey to silk twill, silk weaves can be used for a wide range of applications – blouses, skirts and dresses, naturally enough, but also trims and plackets. Blending silk with other fibres will enhance its natural ability to hold a shape or will produce a material with a greater degree of bulk.

If cotton is the mainstay of a summer collection, wool takes a central role in winter fashion, owing to its warmth and general cosiness. From fine merino lambswool, layered in jumpers and cardigans, or the seductive pampering of cashmere and mohair that feel so luxurious next to the skin, to rugged tweeds and woven woollen suiting that have a high degree of wear-resistance and waterproofing, wool is incredibly varied, both in terms of its sources and in the nature of its woven or knitted textures.

As far as pattern is concerned, wool presents more of a technical challenge than either cotton or silk. One way of creating patterns in wool is Fair Isle knitting, where unused colours are temporarily carried across the back of the work in what are called 'floats'. Another related technique is jacquard knitting or weaving. Much more involved is intarsia, where separate colours in the pattern fit together in a jigsaw fashion. With intarsia, each colour change in a pattern is produced as a separate element and the handwork involved in changing the colours makes this type of production very expensive.

In knitwear, all-over print is applied as a placement to a garment that is sewn together at the shoulder seams and armholes and laid flat on the table. The garment is then finished by sewing along the arms and side seams

Overleaf: Orange wool suit, A/W 2008 with Car print luggage (left) a selection of looks from the same season.

223

and by linking in trims. This method helps the print to appear even, as the pressure applied is consistent.

Producing a small knitwear collection was my entrée into womenswear as well as a natural extension of a lifelong pleasure in knitting as a creative pastime and of my studies in knitted textiles at the Royal College of Art. Knitwear proved to be a good complement to the print side of our collections. The first season we introduced it, we produced a rail of different coloured sweaters in very soft lambswool sourced from a Scottish factory. Each colourway had engineered stripes and colour blocking arranged in different combinations. Other early knitwear designs included jumpers where the sleeves or cuffs were in different colours. As we built up contact with suppliers, we eventually introduced print to our knitwear range.

Leather is a supremely tactile material with the potential to age gracefully and with great character. Vintage bags that show the effects of time often look even better than new, the odd scuff or patch of wear giving them a quirky sense of personality. And, as with many materials, leather is not simply about texture or touch.

Art school training in Dublin and later in London equipped me with an appreciation of the way woven and knitted materials were produced and how they performed, how easy or difficult they were to print and the parameters of the processes involved. Leather was a different story. Until I started to research and investigate leather at the trade fair Lineapelle, I had no idea of how much variation there could be from skin to skin.

What I discovered was that different leathers, from different tanneries or suppliers, might appear superficially very similar, but once you looked closely at them and touched them, the difference was immense. A cheap, or

Stencil illustration of Flower Abacus cardigan and Flower Check bikini, featured in the Telegraph magazine, 2006.

poorly produced, leather feels shoddy and looks flat and even. A good-quality leather, by contrast, is full of character in the grain. The colour will have movement and depth, even when it is a solid shade, and the texture will be supple and resilient, even when the leather is quite thick and substantial. The more attention you pay to the selection of leather, the more discerning you become and the more you come to appreciate its special qualities.

Where possible, we opt for leather that has been coloured with vegetable dyes. The results are infinitely richer and more characterful in appearance than the shades produced by synthetic means. We are also careful to ensure that the leather we use is a by-product and we don't use problematic sources of skins, such as kid or deerskin.

One of the aspects you have to consider as a designer is that using leather entails a great deal of wastage. This naturally arises because skins are not regularly shaped and at times there may be slight flaws that interrupt the surface. A good way of making the most out of your supplies and your investment is to produce small accessories, such as wallets, purses and card cases, with what is left over.

Still-life of Alpine Forest print dress and Ditsy Spot print corduroy bag from A/W 2006.

ready-to-wear

• • • • • • • • •

Designing clothing that will form part of a fashion collection means bearing in mind the mood or personality of the label as a whole. Each piece must also express in some sense the overall theme of a particular season. Within that coherence, however, you need to achieve a certain degree of contrast and variety so that each piece is strong enough to stand on its own. For example, you wouldn't want all the skirts for any given season to share the same silhouette, which may mean producing A-line skirts alongside those that are gathered or pleated. Similarly, we will design tops with different necklines – V-neck, scoop-neck, boat-neck – with a view to how pieces may be layered.

Alongside our main line collection is Olive and Orange, our diffusion range. These designs consist of simple, classic pieces, such as cardigans and dresses, which are supremely easy to wear.

As with colour and print, our inspiration comes from vintage finds of the 1950s, 1960s and 1970s, as seen in photography, films and other sources. Such references may take the form of the detail of a trim or a hemline, or a particular silhouette, but, above all, what we are looking to convey is a sense of youthfulness and optimism. Those postwar decades coincided with a time when young people stopped dressing like their parents, when there was a seismic shift, a 'youthquake' in fashion, from the gamine style of an Audrey Hepburn or a Mia Farrow to the mini-skirted girls of Swinging London and the flower children of the late 1960s. As with all sources of

Photograph of A/W 2010 presentation for London Fashion Week at Somerset House.

231

inspiration, over time such influences become filtered through your own aesthetic until they emerge in the form of a distinctive style or approach. When it comes down to it, I design clothing that I would like to wear myself, or for people who share my own enjoyment in the uplifting and positive quality of colour and pattern.

Our clothing designs are fundamentally simple, with strong symmetrical shapes. Partly that is because pattern is key to what we do and partly that is because we don't like to overcomplicate things. Little twists or surprises come in the detail and trimming – flashes of pattern on a dress lining, for example, or contrasting colours under a cuff, or cute, slightly prim touches, such as high necks and collars.

Above all, we want clothing to be flattering, which means paying careful attention to balance and proportion. If a dress or skirt is to have a big volume, to be gathered or loose, it needs to be short so that more leg is revealed. Sleeve length and waistline must sit at the right level. And the clothing must feel comfortable and pleasant to wear. Even when a dress shape is very structured, for instance, I always like to ensure that the fit is not skin tight, that there is an element of what I call 'hovering', so that you don't feel encased by the fabric but can feel it move or swoosh around you.

The nature of retail means that all clothing must have 'hanger appeal'. There has to be an incentive for someone to pick out a piece and try it on. At the same time, hanger appeal must never override the intrinsic proportion, cut and balance of a design, the way it relates to the human form. We spend a good deal of time ensuring that each design fits the body properly to prevent that sense of disappointment when what looks good on a rail fails to live up to its promise.

Behind the scenes at the shoot for the A/W 2010 lookbook and film.

bags

· · · · · · · · · ·

Choosing a handbag is one way of expressing yourself in a bold and creative way without committing yourself to a particular look from head-to-toe. Simply because you are not wearing it all the time, a bag can serve as a statement piece. Most importantly, you should want to carry it. It should lift your spirits as much as it provides a graphic counterpart or cheerful colour contrast to your outfit.

In practical terms, expectations are high. A bag needs to be sturdy enough to stand up to reasonably regular use and it should include details that simplify life – pockets for tucking away wallets or phones, perhaps a clip where you can fasten your keys to prevent you from having to hunt around for them when they have slipped down to the bottom. It should also be comfortable, which will be a function of its shape and where it sits on the body. As someone who has always carried her bag in the crook of her elbow, I like the look of short handles. Most people, however, prefer to carry their bags on their shoulders or slung across their bodies to keep their hands free. The length of handles or straps affects the proportion of a basic shape: short is not automatically interchangeable with long.

The first stage in the design of a bag is to make rough sketches and explore the potential of different shapes. Once the final designs are chosen, they are drawn at full scale to given an idea of the physical presence of the eventual product. What is particularly enjoyable is fitting in all the details – the pockets, stitch lines, label, zips and closures – to produce a balanced, coherent result.

Car print vinyl luggage and bags shot on location at the Barbican, London, A/W 2008.

Those details that are included should have, as far as possible, a functional reason to be there – I am not a fan, for example, of putting a buckle on a strap that is actually closed by means of a magnet, although there is no reason why magnetic closures should not be concealed by some other means. Over the years we have tried to ring the changes, borrowing ideas for closing bags, for instance, from lateral sources such as the fastenings on men's coats. And it is always nice when there is a hidden element – a bright patterned fabric lining in a leather bag, say – or a bag that can be fully reversed, which gives you two colours or prints for the price of one.

Our label really began with the design of bags. Well before we introduced print, we were producing bags in fashion fabrics, often in tweeds or outerwear fabrics. Next came leather. When we first wanted to produce leather bags, what I was particularly interested in was colour. Because our collections were still tiny at that stage, finding tanneries that would be prepared to supply small quantities in special colours was difficult. Then one day we had a stroke of luck when an agent for an Italian tannery turned up at our door. All our leather is now sourced from Italy.

Early leather designs featured blocks of punched holes and simple graphic contrasts of colour, such as yellow handles on brown bags, orange handles on cream ones, and so on. One season we produced bags with different coloured gussets and stripes; for another collection we used punched holes onto which we would cross-stitch with yarn, a technique we revisited for autumn/winter 2010.

As we introduced print, our bags often became the vehicle for bold or graphic patterns. Now we produce a main line collection, mainly in leather for the winter season, alongside a diffusion range, Etc, which features archive prints

Previous pages: Our label began with the design of bags. These pages show a selection from across the seasons.

that have been recoloured and rescaled, most often in laminated cotton. While our diffusion bags are generally produced in standard shapes and in shoulder and sling versions – with minimal tweaks – our main line is always evolving.

Moving on to the design of luggage has been a natural step. Initially we produced a small range of print-based soft luggage and weekend bags in simple shapes, where the design was printed onto vinyl – one of the patterns that naturally lent itself to that type of application was Car Park. It is important to us to work with specialist factories to produce pieces of luggage that are durable enough to withstand the rough and tumble of baggage handling.

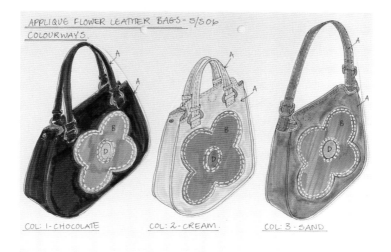

Working drawings of the Applique Flower leather bags from the S/S 2006 mainline collection.

telling the story

· · · · · · · · · ·

Each collection we produce will reflect the mood of the season, with a clear narrative spelled out in colour, pattern and styling. It will also be very focused and edited to make sure each piece is strong.

Consistency is very important to me as a designer and while I know that many customers may well buy only one piece at a time, we always make sure that a collection reads well when it is displayed together, whether at a show or in a shop. Above and beyond the coherence of an individual season, we also take care to ensure that each collection or product range, from diffusion bags to designs for mugs, contributes to our label as a whole.

At the same time, consistency and coherence does not mean sameness or mindless coordination. Everything we design does coordinate, but not in a predictable way and there is always sufficient variety across a collection for a print or individual item to stand on its own. In the beginning we used to arrange our collections by colourway; nowadays they are displayed in looser, more suggestive families of designs to convey how different pieces can work together in different ways.

Achieving that degree of consistency, that design signature, means that you must extend the same degree of control to every type of presentation you make. It is not simply the clothing, bags, accessories or products that must tell the same story, but also the way you display the clothing at a show, the type of props you use, the way you furnish a store, the design of invitations to buyers, and the lookbooks, advertisements, website and film that promote the collection.

A selection of lookbooks that we design and produce to illustrate the mood of each collection.

Above and right: Polariods and sketch used to plan S/S 2003 lookbook image, showing Apple print shirt and Flower Box print bag.

When we were producing our very first collections, the lookbooks that we created each season to show our ranges were shot in houses, cafés and seaside locations that were a little offbeat and retro in style. For the autumn/winter 2007 season, for example, we produced a number of prints that were based around outline shapes of cutlery (flatware), mugs and glassware. We chose a retro café as the location for the fashion shoot. Not only were the colours and mood sympathetic as a background, but the setting also provided a way of suggesting some of the pattern themes.

Now that our label is better known and buyers know what to expect from us, the lookbooks have become more classic in nature, with models posed against a white background to clearly show all the permutations of the collection and how the proportions work on the body. Lately, we have had the opportunity to move into film, which allows us to use the powerful elements of movement and sound to give new dimensions to the stories we tell.

Overleaf: A vintage tiled mural from a 1960s school is the backdrop for the A/W 2004 lookbook.

home

home

. . . .

Creating a house and home provides most people with their greatest opportunity to express their tastes and preferences in a substantial and long-lasting way. Status, for some, will always be an issue, but building surroundings that have character and personality is ultimately more satisfying, rewarding and meaningful. Homes are for living in.

As the backdrop to everyday life, homes have many practical roles to play. Home is where we prepare and cook our meals, where we sleep, eat and wash or otherwise perform the functions necessary for our wellbeing; increasingly, these days, it may also be where we earn our living. The bottom line is that our homes must work well and be fit for all the purposes they serve, which means efficient systems of organization and sensible layouts, so that chores and routines can be tackled with ease. At the same time our homes also have to be places where we feel happy, welcome and comfortable.

Many people are needlessly intimidated when it comes to interior design, both by features in glossy magazines and television programmes that present what appear to be unattainable standards of perfection, and by a fear of making an expensive mistake. All too often that intimidation is expressed by opting for the safe, anonymous and predictable. But turning a house – or a flat or apartment – into a home isn't about spending a fortune or making an extreme fashion statement just because it is the flavour of the moment, it means having the courage of your convictions so that your surroundings truly reflect what you like and what gives you pleasure – an emotional rather

Our living room, with its colourful fireplace tiles, display of vintage vases, Pear Print cushion and Patterned Flower oval rug. Preceding pages: 1970s beach house exterior.

253

than a financial investment. It may be a particular combination of colours, it may be a family of patterns, it may be a style or mood, but the important thing is that it appeals to your taste. An orange vintage light that makes you smile when you turn it on, a family photograph that brings back a happy memory, a warm throw to snuggle up under, a collection of coloured glassware on a windowsill: these are the sort of ingredients that convey the sense of delight and optimism that our homes should be all about.

Much of what has been written about and illustrated in the previous chapters in this book has a direct relevance for home design. You can find sources of inspiration for paint colours, pattern combinations and furnishing fabrics from art, nature and vintage design. You can play about with contrasts of colour, texture and pattern to give depth and character to a decorative scheme. Volume, texture and proportion are just as important elements to consider in the design of soft furnishings as they are in a fashion collection.

And just as personal preferences change and develop, there is no reason why our homes need to stand still. Painting the walls a different colour, changing the bathroom flooring, rearranging displays are all relatively inexpensive and easy ways of putting a fresh face on things, so that our homes retain a sense of vitality.

As outlined in previous chapters, gathering and grouping visual images is a good way of bringing your ideas about decorative or design schemes into focus, whether you are planning to redecorate the living room or are making decisions about your home as a whole. Assembling ideas, in the form of pictures torn out of magazines, swatches of fabric, samples of material or desktop files, may make you feel a little self-conscious at first, but it is a practice that is well worth pursuing and is not really any more taxing or

A selection of our printed mugs shot on location in the Barbican, London.

exposing than taking a magazine clipping along to the hairdressers to show them what sort of haircut you have in mind. Visual reference helps to ground vague preferences in reality.

We don't always have the opportunity or the means to make changes across the board or to treat our homes as a clean slate that can be tackled from top to bottom. Even so, it is a good idea to know in which general direction you are heading, so that you don't end up making decisions in a piecemeal fashion, with the result that your home begins to lack a sense of consistency overall. This is especially important where layouts are more open-plan or where areas directly connect with one another.

Mood board for the Target homeware collection (left) and Multi Flower Spot jacquard towels (above).

mixing old and new

· · · · · · · · · ·

One of the ways to give your surroundings a sense of identity and personality is to mix old with new. Where everything in your home is a period piece or a reproduction of one, it can be like living in a museum or a time warp. On the other hand, exclusively modern interiors can feel a little soulless, like showrooms, or reconstructions of room sets in the pages of a brochure. You need both the freshness of the contemporary and the continuity of the past.

In many homes, history is in-built. Unless you live in a new house or a conversion that has stripped away any hint of what has gone before, the detailing, proportion and layout of your surroundings will carry a reminder of previous ages. Victorian and Edwardian terraces, for example, which make up the bulk of the housing stock in Britain, can be furnished and decorated in a strong contemporary way without any loss of architectural character.

When we bought our house in Clapham, south west London, where we have lived now for seven years, our choice was influenced by the usual factors. Location was high on the list. As our boys were settled in a primary school nearby and our office was in a business centre a short distance away, we wanted to stay in the area. Eventually we were lucky to find a house within our budget that provided us with the space we needed for our growing family. A typical south London terrace, it hadn't been touched in many years and required a significant amount of work, but at least it was structurally sound, with no worrying cracks to indicate serious underlying trouble. Much of what we did to the house consisted of stripping back layers of previous

Family photographs and a vintage lamp in our home (above) and lookbook shot showing a Stem print sofa (below).

decoration – most of the walls were covered in woodchip wallpaper – to reveal its good bones, and making the rooms lighter and brighter. We also tried to save the original features as far as we could. Architectural detail in houses like this is intrinsically tied in with spatial proportions.

Even where detailing is damaged or missing you don't have to be slavish about putting it back in a historically accurate fashion. In our house, the original fireplace tiles were broken and discoloured. Rather than hunt around for reproductions, I bought rectangular tile slips from a tile supplier, two in each colour, and arranged them in stripes, with the main fireplace featuring warm colours and second fireplace cool ones.

Mixing old and new is also a good strategy for furnishing. You do have to exercise a degree of control, however – a jumble of pieces from wildly different periods will simply look as if someone has cleared out their attic and dumped it all in your front room. My own preference is for vintage or retro items from the 1950s onward; putting such pieces together with Victorian- or Edwardian-style furniture, for instance, would be visually indigestible. Some form of theme is necessary to provide an element of consistency. You also need to know where to stop. With this type of approach, simple modern designs, particularly in the case of large, dominant pieces of furniture such as sofas or beds, provide essential breathing space and don't draw attention to themselves, allowing the quirkier or more eclectic items room to speak for themselves.

Vintage pieces are often more affordable than new, particularly if you know where to look. This can be a significant advantage if you are in the process of doing up your first home and are in the position of having to spend money on essential improvements or alterations. Even with the accessibility of sites such as eBay, furnishing a home in this way does take a little more time and effort: it is not a case of visiting the nearest department store and stocking up on a three-piece suite and a dining room set. The reward, however, is not merely economy or a greater degree of originality and character, it is also the joy of discovery, an unexpected lift of pleasure that somehow manages to persist when you bring the piece home and live with it for a time. The overscaled mirror in our living room, for example, is an architrave from a bank, which came from an architectural salvage firm in London and was subsequently glazed. The retro dresser, another piece I am fond of, was in the house when we bought it. Among my favourite pieces is a pair of quirky little side tables with colourful Formica shelves, which have occasionally found their way into the odd photo shoot.

For our label, a successful and rewarding collaboration has been with the British retailer Heal's, a company with a strong design heritage, famous for its contemporary furniture ranges and a progressive force in design since its founding in the early nineteenth century. While many of the products we have designed for Heal's consist of soft furnishings and linen, we have also created a number of pieces of furniture – armchairs, sofas, dining table and chairs, sideboards and cupboards – that have a mid-century-meets-contemporary aesthetic, typically expressed in thin tapering legs and organic curves.

When we were starting out in business we sold to buyers who incorporated our products within their own stores or departments. That progressed to concessions or 'shops within shops', where our merchandise was displayed within the context of someone else's concept of a retail environment. In 2005 we opened our own flagship store in London's Covent Garden, which has since expanded to take in the space next door.

For a designer, a shop of your own is an important opportunity to show a collection in an environment that enables the public to see the whole story. Just as you would present your own taste in the decoration and furnishing of your home, how a shop is decorated, designed and detailed conveys personality, a very specific way of looking at the world.

Nothing could have been less prepossessing than the premises in their original state. The shop used to be a vintage store, for many years a well-known destination for devotees of second-hand or vintage fashion. The whole space was crammed with stuff. We had been looking at another shop further down the road, which I preferred for its frontage, but this shop had greater square footage and our architect reassured me that the space had great potential.

Gerry Taylor, who designed the conversion, has been a friend since Esprit days. As an architect working for the Memphis studio alongside Ettore Sottsass, he had assisted in the design of Esprit's headquarters and shops. Early on in the project it became clear that we would have a good working relationship. His approach was very collaborative and his overall aim was to help us realize our vision for the shop, not to impose a different concept on it. A year later, the shop next door became available and we were able to link the two spaces together on both levels, while retaining the sense that there were four different rooms. A particular feature of the design is the way you can travel or meander through the space, coming in one door, going down the stairs and coming up on the other side.

Although a retail environment is fundamentally a showcase for a range of products or line of clothing, it is also an interior. Incorporating fittings and features that have a home-like quality, such as retro-style lampshades, decorative objects, rugs and seating, helps to contextualize the particular signature of a label. One of the focal points of the shop interior is a lighting installation that consists of different patterned shades hung at varying heights. This is the type of feature that I particularly enjoy designing – and not one I would have been happy to entrust to someone else. Getting it right took trial and error, and it wasn't possible to experiment in situ – instead, I worked on the installation in a workshop before it was finally hung in the shop.

With the shop, we are also able to show a collection in its entirety, and in such a way as to suggest how various outfits could be put together. Buyers who know us particularly for print may not always take the solid or textural pieces we produce as part of our collections. In the shop we can ring the changes and display our designs in all their permutations.

Our prints have been used in a range of applications, from mugs and stationery to bedlinen.

Planning the light installation for our flagship store in Covent Garden.

pattern at home

· · · · · · · · ·

Pattern can never be totally banished from our surroundings: it is there in the most casual arrangement of decorative objects as much as it is present in the character of specific materials, finishes and surfaces. Such instances, what you might call incidental patterning, are one thing; using pattern in a more deliberate and considered way takes more care and thought.

Unless you are going to be focusing exclusively on black and white or neutral and textural prints, introducing pattern inevitably means introducing colour. When you are planning a decorative scheme, it is important not to be too prescriptive or formulaic about it, as that type of approach is often like going shopping for a certain style of dress and not being able to find it. The important thing is to use colours and patterns because you love them, because they mean something to you.

One simple way of getting started is to base a decorative scheme on a favourite piece that you already own, such as a painting, a rug or a sofa. From this 'ready-made' palette you can choose a particular colour to use as a solid, a tone or an accent. Patterns that display some or all of the same colours will have a basic compatibility.

Where any colour is concerned, but particularly background colours that will be used over extensive areas, it can take time to find the right tone or shade, one that gives exactly the effect you are looking for. Those that are edgy and luminous often look very different according to the light conditions in the room at different times of the day. Colours often appear much paler

'Lusk' sofa, part of our Heal's range, with Stem cushions.

on a paint manufacturer's colour chart than they do when they are painted on the wall, where the colour has a tendency to 'mount up' or look more saturated.

As is the case in many London terraced houses, the sitting area in our house runs front to back and is two interconnected rooms. Initially both rooms were painted white, but later I decided to introduce background colour. The olive-green wall colour in the front room was chosen to complement the painting displayed there. The back room was a soothing, restful grey, but of equal tonal value so that the balance flowed between the two spaces. The first time I saw the olive-green walls I was nervous, but when the furniture and furnishings were moved back into the room, all my pieces with their flashes of colour worked beautifully, everything fell into place and the room immediately felt cosier and more intimate.

Perhaps the simplest way of using pattern – and a good way of dipping your toe in the water – is to restrict patterned elements to relatively small-scale applications – such as cushion covers and throws, lampshades or bath linen – or to contain it in some way, for example, by papering the interior of a storage cabinet or shelving unit so that it serves as a slightly hidden element, rather like a lining in a coat.

Using pattern as an accent allows you to build up your confidence gradually, by experimenting with different combinations of designs and different scales of print. Since such small-scale applications are portable, by and large, you can always swap things around or move a scatter cushion or throw to another location if the combination doesn't work quite as well as you had expected.

Treating pattern as a feature or a focal point in a room is a step up from using it as an accent, simply because the scale is greater. A large patterned rug, a sofa upholstered in a bold print, or a wall papered in a large-scale design are all ways of turning pattern into a strong visual statement.

When wallpaper came back into fashion a few years ago, feature walls of print became a popular way of displaying it, very similar to the fashion for painting a single wall in a vivid shade. Like many ideas in interior design, the notion of a 'feature' wall is far from new. In the postwar years, when wallpaper was a popular means of displaying contemporary patterns in the home, the same treatment was rather quaintly known as a 'conversational'.

Any feature or focal point needs a reason to be there and this is particularly true when you are papering a single wall. A feature wall can serve as the backdrop to a furniture arrangement, announce an eating area within an open-plan space, or perform as an overscaled 'headboard' behind a bed. It shouldn't appear stranded in space.

By the same token, when you are isolating a pattern in such a way it is generally more effective if it is large in scale. Small, dense patterns will read more like a texture from a distance.

The richest and liveliest effects are gained by using different patterns in various types of combination. Here it is a question of looking for an element that unifies a collection of disparate designs, as well as playing around with contrasts and opposites.

Unity can be present in a specific combination of colours. Patterns that display the same colours can be remarkably different in type, scale of repeat and motif, and yet still work well together. Quite often, a certain palette of colours will be associated with a specific period in design, so if you opt for vintage prints that date from around the same time, they are likely to have a basic affinity in terms of colour as well as motif.

Another type of unifier is theme. Geometrics, from spots and stripes to checks and plaids, are easy-going in combination because they have the same fundamental mathematical structure. Florals or leaf prints also share a common denominator.

When you are mixing different prints and patterns together it is important to think about basic contrasts of scale, density and texture. Try partnering large-scale motifs with small, dense repeats, linear designs with more representational designs, or crisp graphic patterns printed onto cotton with those have been crocheted or knitted.

Coordination, where the same pattern is extended over a number of different surfaces, needs very careful handling. Too much pattern-matching and there is the risk that foreground and background will dissolve and blur into each other, creating a stifling and claustrophobic effect. Because the eye sees the same thing wherever it looks, excessive coordination can also be oddly lifeless and draining. If you want to repeat a specific design a number of times within a given area, you have to ensure that there are sufficient plain surfaces to serve as intermediaries. A little coordination goes a long way.

Multi Stem print armchair and Blanket Stem cushion shows an effective mix of scale.

surfaces & finishes

· · · · · · · · ·

Wallpaper has long been a vehicle for pattern in the interior. Now that it is back in fashion, after years when plain walls, either coloured or white, have been the norm, it is time to explore its potential. Wallpaper is a particular feature of the interior of our Covent Garden shop, where it is notably used on the wall flanking the staircase, providing a great thread of pattern connecting the upper level with the lower.

Like any other element used in interior decoration, from paint to fabric, wallpaper varies in quality. The best and most expensive versions are generally those that are screen-printed, or hand-printed using wood blocks. The greater the number of colours in a design, the more costly a wallpaper will be. High-quality wallpapers are also thicker and more robust, so they are less likely to tear or crease when they are pasted into place.

In the recent past, wallpaper was often used as a cover-up to disguise superficial irregularities in the surface of a wall, which was one of the ways in which it earned a bad name for itself. Textured wallpaper, such as woodchip, was often used in that way. Good-quality wallpaper, however, deserves to be applied to walls that have been properly prepared, on surfaces that are sound, level and smooth, so that no bumps and ridges interrupt the design. By and large, it also requires professional hanging, particularly those designs featuring large-scale motifs that will require careful placement where a repeat occurs.

When you paint walls and the surrounding trim or detailing, such as woodwork and mouldings, the same colour, the eye naturally skates over any

Red Stem print sideboard with Stem accessories.

The Orla Kiely for Target homeware product range was a great success. The photo (above) was taken for the launch.

imperfections. Wallpaper, however, throws such detailing into high relief, which means that it needs to be crisp, clean-lined and sharp to serve as a foil for the graphic nature of the printed design.

A number of prints that we originally designed for bags or clothing now appear on wallpaper. Not every pattern is suitable for this kind of shift of application. Wallpaper patterns need to have a certain strength and their scale has to be large enough to make a proper impact. That is not to say that a wallpaper pattern has to dominate or jump out at you, but that it has to be robust enough to enhance spatial proportions and read well within its architectural context. A related issue is that the pattern needs to cover the ground evenly, and this is much easier to achieve with a bigger motif or repeat. When I was a child, my bedroom was papered in a brown floral pattern, which I loved. I can remember squinting my eyes and tracing the stripes in the pattern, stripes that were not an intentional part of the design, but that were the result of the way the repeat was arranged so that the ground was not evenly covered.

A pattern that would look huge on clothing can be just the right scale for use on walls. Small, pretty patterns, such as a print we designed one season that featured little hearts composed of flower shapes, I think are too sweet for wallpaper. Wallpaper should never look tentative or wishy-washy.

As previously discussed, when wallpaper first began to be introduced to contemporary homes, it was often in the form of a feature wall. Now that we have become a little more accustomed to it, there is no reason to hold back. A fully papered room has a great sense of intimacy and enclosure. Even a subtle tone-on-tone print featuring simple graphic shapes will express more confidence and flair than plain painted walls. What has yet to be explored is an approach that was a common feature of postwar homes, particularly in the 1940s and 1950s. This was the combination of two contrasting wallpapers on adjacent walls, one a lively and busy design, and the other quieter and more textural.

After walls and ceilings, floors are the largest surface area in the home. In an interior where walls are busy or where there is a lively combination of print and pattern in soft furnishings, it is a good idea for floors to be plain and relatively understated. Running the same type of flooring from area to area is also a way of creating unity or of providing a firm grounding for a decorative scheme.

At the same time, there is great scope for pattern underfoot, where it is much less insistent. We naturally focus on what is ahead, on what is directly in our sightline, not on what we are walking across. That is not to say that floor-level pattern will be overlooked, merely that it is one of the more subtle ways of introducing the vitality of rhythm and repeat.

Many flooring materials naturally incorporate an element of pattern – the rhythm of floorboards is a simple example. More overt patterning can take the form of tile, mosaic, linoleum and rugs. Areas that are self-contained, such as bathrooms, often benefit from the lift of pattern or colour on the floor. In our house, a bright red stripe painted up the wooden stairs creates a vivid pathway that leads the eye onward.

Thinking laterally can also provide inspiration. Once, while I was walking along the street, observing the small, square paving stones with raised spots that are put at pedestrian crossings to aid the blind, I thought how well these would work as paving stones in our garden. I contacted the firm that supplied them and created an interesting patio space very economically.

Following pages: Wallpaper collection: Striped Petal, Rowan Tree, Tulip, Multi Stem and Geranium Stem.

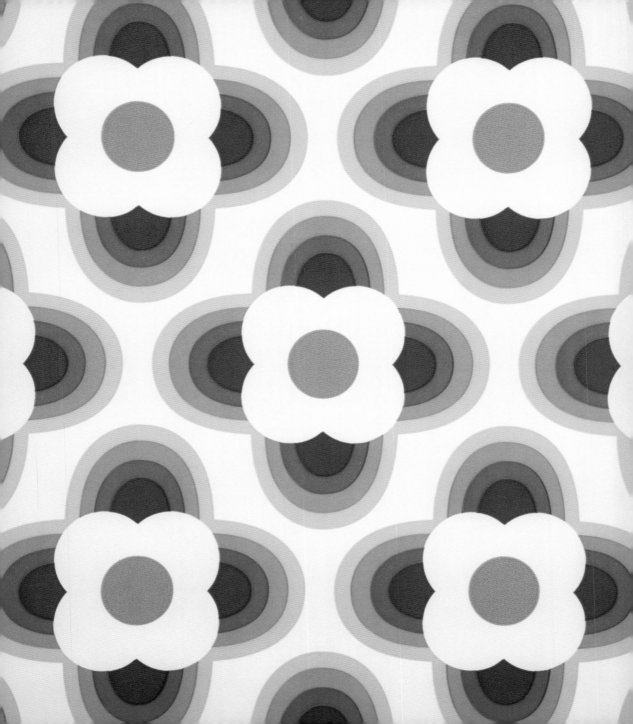

Snapshots from design blogs showing the way different people have used Stem wallpaper in their homes.

Although patterned vintage textiles are relatively easy to find, the same isn't true of vintage carpet or other softer flooring materials – probably because people get rid of them only when they are fairly worn out. In the 1970s I remember my grandmother making hand-tufted rugs from kits, and at home we had a carpet with a sculpted floral pattern in a diamond repeat on which we played hopscotch; we also had some fairly mad floor tiles in the kitchen. When we bought our present house, most of the floors were covered in patterned carpet, which we disposed of. Now I wish I had salvaged the best bits.

Soft furnishings of all descriptions, from towels to bed covers, from curtains to covered headboards, are ideal for the display of pattern and provide the opportunity to experiment creatively with different types of fabric. I love to sew, but you don't have to be particularly adept at it to make simple items, such as a blind or shade, or a gathered curtain, from whatever remnants you have collected. Vintage scarves or old Fair Isle knitwear, for example, can make strikingly original cushion covers. From blogs we know that plenty of people have had fun adapting our fabric to different uses – a Stem pillowcase being used to make a bag or a purse, or curtains fashioned out of bedding.

Fabric in the interior is all about comfort. Upholstery and cushions support the body, bed and bath linen feel good next to the skin, woollen throws add warmth on a cold night. Comfort, however, is not simply about touch or the tactile properties of different materials, it also has a visual aspect. It is important to get the balance right. Too much fabric and an interior can begin to feel swaddled and smothered; too little and it will look clinical and unyielding, no matter how comfortable it actually is.

Dressing a home with fabric calls for clean lines and strong shapes. I am not a huge fan of slipcovers or voluminous drapery – I like to see the structure

Overleaf: The house designed by architect Ivor Berresford in 1958 was the location for our S/S 2007 shoot.

and form of furniture, not hide it, which means tailored upholstery and a minimum of trimming. Piping, for example, lends crispness to a cushion cover, whereas excessive embellishment blurs its lines.

Graphic patterns at different scales add visual delight to household linen. Because these items are changed regularly, you can introduce a new look every time you do the washing. One week you may be in the mood for a large-scale print in bright colours; another time you might prefer something more muted. We have used Stem in several ways on duvet covers, for example, from a large multicoloured version, to a white tonal jacquard weave, to a tiny version where the repeat becomes almost a texture. Printing onto towelling adds a different dimension because of the piled nature of the fabric; equally effective are jacquard weaves and sculpted designs, where the pattern takes the form of a relief.

The Multi Stem print even appears on our range of doormats for Heal's.

285

display

. . . .

Display is a way of sharing your taste and expressing yourself in your surroundings. Whatever you leave out on view in your home – photographs, paintings, vases or decorative objects – does not have to be intrinsically valuable or precious, but it must mean something to you, otherwise there is no point in it being there. Quite ordinary household objects make intriguing displays, particularly when they are grouped together. Bright enamelled colanders hanging from a rail, stripy storage jars or an array of patterned mugs are the kind of everyday items that can provide a great deal of visual pleasure for next to nothing.

Recently, we were approached by the American retailer Target to produce a range of homewares. What was especially rewarding about this collaboration was that we were allowed complete control over the designs that were used. After we agreed the basic products on which the designs would be displayed, we played around with the scale of the patterns and tweaked the colours to suit the various different applications. Although the company was initially leaning toward a palette based around various shades of blue, which it believed was more immediately commercial, we were able to convince them to work with greens, oranges and browns alongside the blues for a more mix-and-match approach. The range, which included storage jars, plates, bowls, trays, mugs and vases, was promoted very cleverly by Target in a series of blogs in the run-up to the launch, and sold out almost immediately.

Many of us are magpies, drawn to collect families of similar objects regardless of how valuable they are, and displaying such objects together is

This vintage cabinet, one of my favourite pieces, was in our house when we bought it.

On display: Family photographs and vintage vases in my home.

a good way of making a quantity of things read as a single unit. Otherwise, if you scatter them about from place to place, you run the risk of making a room look unnecessarily cluttered or bitty.

I am particularly drawn to vintage and retro objects that display a strong use of colour or a sculptural organic form. While each piece may be eye-catching in its own right, grouped together they are even more powerful. Because our living room is rather narrow, we added shelves at a high level to make the space seem a little wider, and these shelves are largely devoted to display. Other good places for collections include mantelpieces, cabinets, sideboards or any surface where there is an element of containment.

Lighting always helps to bring out the particular qualities of items on display. Wall lights above the shelves in our living room highlight the form of the vases and accentuate their colours. Backlighting is especially effective when you are displaying glass – coloured glass placed on a windowsill so that light shines through it looks incredibly luminous. Side lighting grazes the surface of an object and reveals its texture and form.

Our house has undergone a number of transformations. Moving from white walls to background colour was a big shift, and I have changed the colour again in some rooms. The overscaled headboard that conceals storage space in our bedroom has been white, deep blue and is currently patterned in our Tulip print. My husband jokes that I have decorated the living room eight times, and while this may be an exaggeration, I do like to try new things.

Most of us don't move the furniture around once we have settled on an arrangement that works, and few people redecorate as often as I do. Displays, though, are easy to change. There is no better way of putting a fresh face on things and giving the eye something new to look at and take pleasure in.

Overleaf: Photographs of my kitchen from the Japanese magazine by Harumi Kurihara.

昨年開店したばかりのショップ。
日本でも人気のバッグをはじめ、靴、傘、ショッピングカートなどの雑貨類からセーター、スカート、パンツなどの新コレクションまで、オーラさんのすべてがそろいます。

Orla Kiely　オーラ・カイリー
31 Monmouth Street, London, WC2H 9DD
☎ 020 7240 4022
http://www.orlakiely.com　無休

イギリスでも家庭と仕事を
両立させている女性は尊敬されます。

つらいこともいっぱいあったけれど、子育てと仕事の両方をがんばってきてよかった。私自身、人として成長したし、夫、娘、息子、それぞれともいい関係が作れたと思う。そんな今の私の心境をオーラさんに伝えると「私も同じ。間違いなく子どもがいちばん大事ですが、どちらか片方という人生は考えられません。イギリスでも家庭と仕事を両立させている女性は尊敬されます。自分がやりたいことをあきらめないで、やり続けることがすてきな女性の条件ではないでしょうか」。肩ひじ張らず夫と協力して、仕事も家庭も楽しんでいるオーラさん。その幸福感が家中に、作品にあふれ出ているようでした。

細長いスペースを生かしたキッチン。壁にはふたりの息子さんのおけいこスケジュールを書き込んだボードが。テーブルクロスの葉っぱのパターンは、オーラさんのトレードマークともいえるおなじみの柄。懐いやすく見た目も楽しいキッチンで）

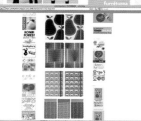

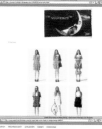

blogs

• • • • • • • • •

As a creative forum where images can be gathered, designed and posted, blogs are an endless source of amazement and inspiration to me. Immediate and instantly accessible, they serve as a platform on which anyone and everyone can express their likes and dislikes, share their interests and passions and interact with the world.

It is a total compliment and such a thrill to see my work displayed and discussed in cyberspace, the happy reactions it provokes and the impact it has on others who share my taste. I also find plenty to inspire me in the other images that may have caught a blogger's eye.

Seeing how people interpret pattern and colour in their own homes is always interesting. Whether it's a tablecloth we designed for Target used to reupholster a chair, or our Stem print wallpaper running up the stairs or pasted to cupboard doors, there's so much creativity and invention out there.

And this willingness to share a particular vision isn't restricted to homeware. In many blogs people report on what's happening with their favourite designers, feed back on catwalk shows and presentations and react to the arrival of a new season. For us, this is an excellent way to observe our successes, and pick up on what our friends and customers are responding to as they tag, post and upload their favourite looks. It's a powerful medium where directness and honesty override all else. Genuine and endlessly creative, the blogger's voice is loud and clear.

A selection of blog pages featuring our products, with immediate comments and reactions.

Snapshots from selected blogs showing how people have used Flower Blossom wallpaper in different ways in their homes.

afterword

• • • • • • • • •

Taking on this book, a project of epic proportions, has been immensely cathartic. Delving into the past, gathering and deciphering material – boxes and boxes of it – has made me smile as memories have crept back into my consciousness. My career so far has been a journey in pattern that I never felt I planned, as I rushed along busily from one season to another. My life continues to be hectic, but sometimes it is useful to take stock and step away from the creative maelstrom. Sometimes you have to stop the carousel and get off. This project provided that moment for me, both to look back and to look forward.

Even though at the time it wasn't evident, it now seems to me that there has been a pattern to my development. Unexpectedly, I found a voice, which became clearer and stronger over time. There is no clear dividing line between where inspiration ends and hard work begins, but there has been plenty of both. Further, when I reassess my evolution and the designer that I have become, I can begin to visualize where this journey will take me next. As a company, we have created a brand that reflects not just our aesthetic but also our values. Increasingly, I find myself considering the consequences and impact of producing products for an already cluttered world. My hope is that I am always associated with products that will be valued, cherished and not discarded.

Having completed this journey of rediscovery, I realize that you cannot control the emotional responses and effects that pattern generates. Just like listening to music or reading poetry, the order, the rhythm and the flow stimulates the creative inner person and somehow inspires.